Bible Fun Stuff

FOR AGES 9-11

X-perience It!

David C Cook
transforming lives together

X-PERIENCE IT!
Published by David C. Cook
4050 Lee Vance View
Colorado Springs, CO

David C. Cook Distribution Canada
55 Woodslee Avenue, Paris, Ontario, Canada N3L 3E5

David C. Cook U.K., Kingsway Communications
Eastbourne, East Sussex BN23 6NT, England

David C. Cook and the graphic circle C logo
Are registered trademarks of Cook Communications Ministries.

Written by Julia Taves
Cover Design: BMB Design/ Scott Johnson
Interior Design: TrueBlue Design/Sandy Flewelling
Illustrations: Guy Wolek

Scripture quotations, unless noted, are
from the HOLY BIBLE, NEW INTERNATIONAL VERSION.
1973, 1978, 1974 by International Bible Society.
Used by permission of Zondervan. All rights reserved.

ISBN 978-1-4347-6717-2

First Printing 2009
Printed in the United States

1 2 3 4 5 6 7 8 9 10

David C Cook
transforming lives together

TABLE OF CONTENTS

INTRODUCTION

Get those lessons off the page and into the hands of your most energetic students! Simulations and role-playing activities work so well with upper elementary children because they challenge old perceptions about learning. Forget about recycling old-school methods of teaching biblical concepts—*X-perience It!* activities will deepen your students' knowledge of God and drive them to discover why things work so well God's way.

Each role-play gives students the power of choice within set guidelines. And since what they choose directly affects the outcome of each unique simulation, your students will internalize biblical truth as they not only hear and see, but actively improvise to overcome chance obstacles and respond to others' choices.

HOW TO USE THIS BOOK

The activities in this book can be done in any order and easily fit into any curriculum. Simply use the Scripture and Topic Index on page 110 to match a simulation with the lesson you're teaching. These activities also can be used as alternate Step Three activities in several curriculum lines: David C. Cook Bible-In-Life, Echoes, LifeLINKS to God, College Press, Reformation Press, Wesley, Anglican, and The Cross. If you have one of these lines, look through the Correlation Chart on page 111 and find the activity geared to your lesson. You'll use this new activity instead of one of the other Step Three activities listed in your teacher's guide. This book, when combined with *Hot Crafts for Cool Kids,* will give you a full year's worth of Step Three replacement activities for the elementary age group.

The first page of each activity in *X-perience It!* opens with a Bible Background giving you some information about the Scripture for the day. The next page has Teacher Tips including preparations needed and Supplies Needed. On the final two pages for each activity you will find the Setup, Rules to Live By, and Simulation. The Analyzing the Situation discussion questions will help your students fully process the biblical truth of the game.

During each simulation, players will adopt and act out a variety of roles with different ideas, goals, and backgrounds. Actions will be determined by the players' choices. At the beginning of each activity, read the situation's Setup to explain the parameters of time, roles, background, characters, and setting. The rules for each simulation should be discussed and then clearly posted for students to refer to while playing out the activity.

Helpful Hints:

○ Provide a room or space where kids can move around freely.

○ Emphasize kids putting themselves in someone else's shoes and thinking like someone else.

○ Be prepared to guide students while encouraging their own creativity and flexibility.

○ Always post the rules in a place students can refer to easily.

○ Create a signal, such as a unique phrase or sound, to get students' attention to move on to question time or signal that the simulation is complete.

HEY! YOU DID THAT ON PURPOSE!

A show and tell simulation illustrates God's design-and-create nature.

Bible Basis:
Genesis 1:6–13

Memory Verse:
How many are your works, O LORD! In wisdom you made them all; the earth is full of your creatures.
Psalm 104:24

BIBLE BACKGROUND

If you walk into your kitchen and see a beautifully decorated birthday cake on the counter with the words "Happy Birthday" on it, you might think, "Where did that cake come from and who made it?" Does it cross your mind that the cake pulled itself together out of the flour and sugar from your cupboard? You know that someone created the cake for a specific purpose. You see the designer's work and appreciate the maker. You feel good because it was designed specifically with someone in mind!

While we can combine existing elements and ideas to make new things, only God has the power to make something from nothing. The incredible order and symmetry and beauty of creation clearly demonstrate God's creative wisdom. From today's Scripture and others, we can clearly see how our wonderful world reflects God's planning and purposes. We know from Genesis 1 that the entire universe came into existence through the expressed will of the eternal God.

In today's lesson we see how animals were created according to God's care and sovereign design. As you prepare for the lesson, ponder how much thought God our Creator put into this world. Your own enthusiasm will no doubt affect your students' way of looking at their Creator.

TEACHER TIPS

○ This simulation focuses on God's design. Look for ways to direct discussion toward God's amazing creation and the way we're made. This is a great opportunity to encourage your tweens in the unique way God designed each of them.

○ Prepare bags of supplies ahead of time so kids can use their time creating instead of gathering. Use any available supplies from the list provided or from your own imagination.

○ Consider writing the "Rules to Live By" on a separate poster board or whiteboard for students to see during the simulation.

SUPPLIES NEEDED

For the teacher:

○ Large brown paper grocery sack

○ Slips of paper

○ Pen

○ Small brown bag

For the class:

Zip-top bags, 1 per student, with at least three items in each:

○ Wire, foil, clay

○ Chenille wire, paper, glue

○ Wire, cardboard, beads

○ Clay, chenille wire, string

○ Chenille wire, string, beads

○ String, tape, paper

○ Paper, marker, egg carton

○ Pictures, craft sticks, glue

○ Wire, paper, toilet paper rolls

○ Tape, cardboard, foil

Note: You may duplicate more bags depending on how many students are in your class. Materials may vary depending on supplies available, and you don't need to include a large amount of each item in each bag. The idea is to have a variety of materials available.

Setup

○ You will need one bag per student with at least three items in each. Hide these smaller bags in a large brown grocery bag so students can't see the supplies ahead of time.

○ Prepare a small bag of folded slips of paper with Xs and Os on them. You will need one slip per student. Try to have an even number of each. On the papers with an X, include these instructions: "You will have 10 minutes to design something special out of your materials!" On the papers with an O, include these instructions: "For 10 minutes, just enjoy playing with your materials—don't create anything with a specific purpose out of them!"

Rules to Live By

① You must use the materials you're given.

② Follow your written directions.

Simulation

This simulation gets students thinking about the difference between something fashioned with a purpose versus something that randomly appeared.

We see God's design and purpose of order in all of creation around us. The way the planets and stars stay in place is just one of the many amazing designs God created. In this activity, you'll get to be a master designer. Let's see what you can create!

Pretend you're inventors at a convention. You've been given a mystery bag of supplies. One bag may include string, tape, and paper. Another bag might contain wire, foil, and clay. When I say go, you'll have 10 minutes to follow the instructions on your paper.

Ask students to choose a slip of paper from the small brown bag with either an X or an O on it. Students with the X are secretly instructed to create an object with specific purpose and design. Students with an O just randomly play with the materials, NOT creating anything with a purpose. At the end of 10 minutes, have each person present his or her work. Those who were instructed to create something with a purpose should explain to the class what they've created, while the "random play-ers" will have nothing new to show.

ANALYZING THE SITUATION

○ **How can you tell if something was designed on purpose at our convention?** *(It has order or a design that's evident.)*

○ **If God could do a "show and tell" about His creation, what would He say?** *(It's good, it has a purpose, and I made it!)*

○ **Where do we see God's design in creation around us?** *(Answers will vary, but might be the water cycle, planets staying in place, snowflakes, peacock feathers, etc.)*

○ **How did you feel when others saw your design in your creation?** *(pleased, happy, etc.)*

○ **How do you think God feels when we marvel at what He made?** *(honored, pleased, loved, etc.)*

SUPER STATUES!

A role-playing activity helps children see how valuable they are to God.

BIBLE BACKGROUND

Do you prefer a rainy day snuggling by a fire with a good book or a sunny day playing tennis outside? Are you a person who likes to be in charge or someone who loves to follow? Are your eyes blue or green or brown? Are you tall or of average height? The answers to these questions will differ from person to person because each of us was created with unique traits and characteristics.

When God created Adam, His special creation was distinctly different from the animals. Though we share some things in common with certain members of the animal kingdom, only people are created in God's image. In Psalm 139:14, the psalmist praises God for His marvelous creation: "I praise you because I am fearfully and wonderfully made; your works are wonderful, I know that full well."

We were each created to be unique and special, with the purpose to glorify God. The many differences among human beings are not random, but given by a loving creator who provides for all of His creation.

Students at this age desperately need to know that their specific qualities are special and have value to others. Look for the creative differences God made in the kids in your class today. Encourage each one, and point out how blessed you are to see the ways God created him or her. Use this lesson to affirm the distinctiveness of God's design in every student. Thank God for each unique person He has created!

TEACHER TIPS

○ This activity gives your wiggly kids a lot of freedom to move and show off. But encourage them to wait their turn so each student can be the center of attention at different times. (Note: This activity may be familiar to some of your students as a variation on the classic children's game, "Swing the Statue.")

○ Some traits might be harder than others to act out, so you might want another leader to pose as the museum owner rather than a student. This way, he or she can preview the trait choices before class starts and better interpret the clues given by the statue.

SUPPLIES NEEDED

○ Basket or hat to hold slips of paper
○ Pen
○ Paper

You may use the following list of talents or character traits for your statues, or you may want to create your own list. If you have more than 10 kids, duplicate as needed since each statue will still be unique in its actions.

Traits:
Musically talented
Athletic
Intelligent
Able to build things
Funny
Compassionate or kind
Strong
Organized
Friendly
Shows leadership

SETUP

You need at least four players for this imaginative game. One player is the archeologist, one is the museum owner, and the rest are statues. These positions may be rotated after each round of the game. The archeologist will draw traits out of a hat and show them to each of the statues privately. The museum owner will try to guess each statue's trait when the stutue begins to pantomime.

RULES TO LIVE BY

Discuss these rules before starting. You may want to write them out and post them at the front of the class.

① When the archeologist spins you, you must stay in the position in which you land until your "on button" is pushed.

② Your character trait must be kept secret from everyone except you and the archeologist.

③ You must find a way to convey the talent or character trait that the archeologist shares with you. The museum owner will try to figure out your talent based on your pantomime or actions. You may act, but may not speak or make noise.

SIMULATION

At one time you were no bigger than a tiny dot. You began as a single cell and divided inside your mom as you grew. Even when you were that small, many things about you had already been decided: whether you were a boy or girl; what color your eyes would be; and how many toes and fingers were on your feet and hands! When God created you, He designed you in a special way.

Imagine opening your eyes and finding yourself a statue in a strange museum full of other statues. You look around at the many wonders and unusual objects. How you got to this place is uncertain, but you realize that you're very different from the other statues around you.

Today you're going to pretend that each statue in this museum is one of God's creations—a kid just like you! You won't know what special gift God gave you until the archeologist "discovers" you! He'll do this by pressing your "on button" (your nose) and showing you what trait you have. At that time, you'll have to act out that gift the best you can. For example, if the archeologist presses your nose and shows you a paper with the word *athletic*, then you'll come to life and possibly act out a sport or athlete in motion.

To make this more interesting, the archeologist will spin each statue around and let you go. The players who are statues must freeze where they've fallen or

landed until their "on button" is pushed. The museum owner, who doesn't know what your unique trait might be, will try to guess based on the clues you give him when you come to life.

Are you ready to try it?

ANALYZING THE SITUATION

○ **Was it difficult to act out the trait you were given? Why or why not?** *(Answers will vary.)*

○ **What was unique about your statue?** *(I was the only one who could sing really well, my traits were shown more on the inside than the outside, etc.)*

○ **If God created people in His image, what do you think God is like?** *(He is creative, capable of love, etc.)*

○ **How much do you think God cares for us? What evidence do we have that demonstrates His care?** *(Answers will vary.)*

IT'S ALL MINE, BABY!

A shopping expedition exposes our true motives.

Bible Basis:
Genesis 4:1–16

Memory Verse:
"Those whom I love I rebuke and discipline."
Revelation 3:19

BIBLE BACKGROUND

Cain worked the soil. Abel took care of sheep. Cain did his duty and nothing more. Abel went out of his way to please God. Cain was jealous of the approval Abel received and resentful of his own admonition from God, thus opening the door for anger. Abel was righteous and longed to please God. This is a picture of duty versus devotion.

Today we often face similar conflicts. Our gifts and time should be offered from a willing heart—not from a sense of obligation. Having an intimate relationship with God and knowing what pleases Him should be the motive behind our actions. How can we learn to live and give out of devotion rather than duty?

Just as King David said, we should not offer to God something that costs us nothing. A good attitude is hard to muster up some days, especially when we find our efforts being constantly corrected. Consider how you respond to correction: is it with humility or with resentment, as Cain exhibited? God desires for each of us to have a teachable heart.

TEACHER TIPS

○ As a teacher, you have the opportunity to model for students giving that pleases others and pleases God. Help them understand that God desires for us to know what pleases Him most and give accordingly. This will happen naturally when we know God and listen to His voice.

○ It would be beneficial to have a coworker manage the store in order to keep things moving at a quick pace. Possibly set a timer and give students a couple of minutes to shop before the next group gets a chance.

○ It will be easiest to use paper money and have everything in the store cost one dollar. This will make the activity move quickly as the person managing the store will not have to give change, and everyone will receive the same number of items.

○ Dollar stores make great places to shop for the kinds of items listed below. If you don't have a fund to purchase such items, ask parents to donate new or gently used things they have at home.

○ Students will tend to want to focus on the store items, but the lesson goal will be for them to understand that what counts most is what they decide to give away at the end.

SUPPLIES NEEDED

○ Pretend paper money (at least 3 dollar bills for each student)

○ Pretend coins for storekeepers to make change (if necessary)

○ Items for students to purchase in the store such as:

> Books (This is what the teacher really wants the students to buy.)
> Pens
> Bookmarks
> Candy
> Small balls
> Necklaces
> Carabineers
> Bracelets
> Sunglasses
> Small stuffed animals

○ *Optional:* timer

SETUP

○ Set up a table with items for purchase such as toys, candy, books, etc. Show everyone the table and give each person $3.00 in play money to spend any way he or she wishes.

○ Choose at least three people to be store workers. Privately let them know that their job is to get kids to buy anything but the books. Suggest they make up a selling pitch for items or even lower the prices on items to practically give them away for free.

RULES TO LIVE BY

Discuss these rules before starting. You may want to write them out and post them at the front of the class.

① You may only spend $3.00 at the store.

② Once something is purchased, you may not return it or change your mind.

③ You may keep whatever you purchase for yourself.

SIMULATION

In everyday life we strive to please God by doing what's right. Finding out what pleases God is most important, but sometimes our own desires can get in the way.

While we're doing this simulation, see if you can figure out how our choices affect the outcome of the experience. Bring a few kids at a time to purchase something from the table. As their teacher, tell them that you hope they enjoy the things you have made available for them to purchase.

As students are purchasing things, drop hints such as, "These books are really cool. I think the books would be a special thing to have." Or, "The book choices look fun." You're trying to determine who notices what's most important to you and is willing to buy it to give to you as a gift.

Now that all of you have had a chance to shop, each of you must bring one thing you're willing to give back to me as your gift. Note which students were paying attention to your hints and gave you the item you really wanted (books) and which students simply gave you anything they had available.

ANALYZING THE SITUATION

○ **What was the best thing you bought?** *(Answers will vary.)*

○ **How did you decide what to give your teacher? How did you know what would please your teacher most?** *(I heard him/her mention what he/she really liked, I didn't know—I just gave something that I didn't care that much about, etc.)*

○ **How did you feel when others gave their gifts?** *(I felt happy for my teacher, I felt jealous that mine wasn't as special, etc.)*

○ **Do you remember the story of Cain, who compared himself to his brother rather than focusing on what God wanted? What was Cain's attitude when God corrected him?** *(He was jealous and became angry and resentful.)*

○ **Why is it important to know what pleases God most?** *(So we can honor and please Him.)*

PLAN-IT PLANET

An out-of-this-world view teaches us about God's provision and saving grace.

Bible Basis:
Genesis 8:1—9:17

Memory Verse:
It is by grace you have been saved, through faith—and this not from yourselves, it is the gift of God.
Ephesians 2:8

BIBLE BACKGROUND

At times a good rain is refreshing, but constant rain for 40 days might cause anyone to complain. After Noah and his family spent 40 days on the ark with all those animals in the unending rain, it was still about another 11 months until the floodwaters completely receded.

As the eight people and the animals left the ark on Mt. Ararat, they had the opportunity for a fresh start; but rebuilding would take massive amounts of work. Before he began that work, Noah built an altar to worship and praise God for keeping him and his family safe.

God not only kept them safe, but also made awesome promises and guaranteed He would never judge the earth in that way again. Isn't it just like God to go beyond what we need and provide comfort and assurance? God gave us a visible reminder of His promise when He painted a rainbow to show His amazing grace and love.

Noah and his family focused on the promises of God as they began to rebuild their lives. We too can be encouraged that God will provide and save us from our needless worries and fears if we dwell on His unending promises. Encourage your tweens to look at God's promises as He has provided a way of salvation for each of us.

Teacher Tips

○ Guiding students through a cooperative learning exercise can help them understand how others may feel. It's important for you to use this simulation to get kids thinking about God's provision, promises, and undeserved favor.

○ As you facilitate, be sure to encourage each student to play a part in the thinking process.

○ It's good to target each student's ability to help each work cooperatively. For example, choose the timid student to be the writer for the group or enlist the artist to draw the home plans, and so forth.

○ Ask questions as you go to stimulate students' thinking. What would happen if you cut down all the fruit trees to build homes? How does the colder weather affect your food supply? Who would help you build the homes? In what ways can you take care of the animals on the planet?

○ Emphasize the fact that God has provided not only for our physical needs, but also for our salvation. Be prepared to answer questions about salvation if students have them. Encourage those who show interest in knowing Christ to talk to you or another Christian adult after the lesson.

Supplies Needed

○ Paper
○ Pencils

SETUP

Your whole class has landed on an alien planet. Divide students into four groups. (The size of your class will determine how many per group.) Give each group a job to do when they get off the spaceship. Give each group paper and a pencil to journal ideas.

RULES TO LIVE BY

Discuss these rules before starting. You may want to write them out and post them at the front of the class.

① Your new planet has vegetation and a few fruit trees.

② The only people on the planet are the ones who came in your spaceship.

③ Although some animals are smaller than we see on our planet, two of every kind of animal lives on your new planet.

④ There is a deep lake in every crater.

⑤ The seasons are the same as on Earth, except winters are extremely cold.

⑥ It's springtime when you arrive.

SIMULATION

The earth must suddenly be evacuated (meteor shower, trash overtaking the earth, or anything outrageously dramatic you can dream up). **Your dad was building an experimental spaceship in your barn out back. You and your friends thought this was ridiculous, but you went along with it because, after all, he is your dad. It used to seem silly, but now this spaceship has offered hope for escape.**

Traveling in space has been exciting but exhausting. Eating freeze-dried food, living in cramped quarters, and living in zero gravity can be irritating at times. But you're safe for the time being. Even though your situation is hard, you're thankful that you've survived.

You look ahead and see a planet in the distance. Could this be your new home? As you land, many thoughts go through your head. How do you know it's safe to get out? What will you eat? How will you survive? As you take on the role of space survivors, these are the questions you'll figure out today.

Each of you has been assigned a different group with different tasks. I'm going to tell you what your group's job will be in order to help everyone survive. Are you ready?

Share with each group their specific tasks, instructing them that they'll have 10 minutes to figure out their plans.

Group #1: Food Planning

Where will you find it? What will you eat? How will you prepare it? How will you store it for the coming winter months?

Group #2: Location
Where will you live? What will provide your water supply? Do you need to make a map of the area? Is this the best spot to live?

Group #3: Church and Worship
How will you thank God for safety? How will you remember His provision? What kind of altar will you build? What are your plans for worshiping God together?

Group #4: Shelter
What materials will you use to build a house? What will it look like? How will you protect yourselves from the cold?

After the 10 minutes are up, gather students to share and discuss their plans.

ANALYZING THE SITUATION

- **How would you feel if this really happened to you and your family?** *(Answers will vary.)*

- **How were you able to survive? What was already provided for you?** *(animals, vegetation, water, natural materials, etc.)*

- **How did you use these resources?** *(Answers will vary depending on the group plans.)*

- **When Noah experienced a similar crisis, how did God provide for him and his family?** *(God gave them the animals, natural resources like vegetation, a future promise of protection, etc.)*

- **What are some ways God provides for you?** *(Answers will vary.)*

- **How does it make you feel to know God has provided not only for our physical needs, but also for our salvation through His Son, Jesus?** *(Answers will vary.)*

STAND ALONE

A version of "Simon Says" showcases individual integrity.

Bible Basis:
Genesis 13:11–12; 18:1–5, 16–33; 19:1–29

Memory Verse:
Be alert and always keep on praying for all the saints.
Ephesians 6:18b

BIBLE BACKGROUND

Abraham cared deeply about his nephew Lot who lived in Sodom, a town filled with evil and violent people. Because of Abraham's deep compassion, he became an intercessor between the people of Sodom and God. Abraham knew God was merciful, so he pleaded with God not to destroy the evil city.

When three heavenly visitors appeared to Abraham, he bowed down and hurried to serve them the best he had in order to honor them. Two of the visitors were angels and one was called the Lord Himself. Abraham exhibited extraordinary humility, especially considering the fact that he was a great man in the region.

Abraham boldly interceded with God—not once but six times—to show mercy to Sodom and to Lot and his family. The Word admonishes us to be bold when asking for the desires of our hearts (see Matt. 20:31–32; Luke 11:5–9; 18:4–5). Not only did Abraham intercede, but he was also the only one standing between God and the complete destruction of a town—and all the people in it.

God promises throughout His Word that He will hear our prayers and answer. Keep alert to pray for those kids in your class today who may need you to intercede for them. God is ready to listen.

TEACHER TIPS

○ Since the "secret student" will need to follow a different set of instructions, be sure to select a responsible and confident person—not necessarily the class clown.

○ Keep the game moving quickly and maintain control, even though it's fast-paced and lively. It will be important to go over the rules and emphasize need to follow directions.

SUPPLIES NEEDED

○ Index cards (1 for each student)

○ Pen

Create instruction cards by writing the following directions on index cards for all but one student:

A—Clap your hands behind your back
B—Sing "Jingle Bells"
C—Do 10 jumping jacks
D—Shout your favorite color

Write the following different directions for one student:

A—Clap your hands above your head
B—Sing "Silent Night"
C—Jump on one foot
D—Shout your least favorite animal

SETUP

○ Give the idea that you're playing a "Simon Says" type game, but this is actually an activity demonstrating that it's hard when you stick out from the crowd.

○ Hand out an instruction card to each student. One card will be different from the rest. Don't let any of the students know that one is not like the others. (Be sure to give this card to the student who will carefully follow these directions, even though the others are doing something different. After all the students have their cards, begin quickly before they have time to compare notes.

RULES TO LIVE BY

Discuss these rules before starting. You may want to write them out and post them at the front of the class.

① You must follow the exact directions on your card.

② You will be given 10 seconds to follow the directions given.

③ You may not talk unless directed to do so in your directions.

④ You must not show your directions to anyone else.

SIMULATION

Sometimes it's hard to follow directions because we're distracted or confused, or maybe we're just not paying attention! Many parents think it may be difficult for kids your age to follow exact directions, but I'm sure you all are different. I believe you can rise to the challenge.

Let's see if you can take a challenge and follow directions exactly. When I say, "A!" immediately follow the first direction labeled A on your index card. When I say, "B!" immediately follow that direction, and so on. Try to follow me no matter how fast I go, or what order I say the directions. Do your best to not mess up. Any questions?

Begin to play this version of Simon Says, allowing your students to consult their cards to complete their actions. Change the order of the letters or vary the speed—whatever you choose to keep the game interesting. Of course, one of the students will do something different from the rest, and the others will start noticing.

After playing the game for a short time, bring students together for class discussion.

ANALYZING THE SITUATION

○ **On a scale of 1–10, how would you rate yourself on following directions?** *(Answers will vary.)*

○ **Did any of you find it difficult to do exactly what was written on the card?** *(Answers will vary.)*

○ Specifically ask the student with the different directions this question: **How did you feel having a different set of directions from everyone else? Did you feel like questioning the teacher?** *(Most will admit feeling out of place or different.)*

○ **When have you ever had to do something to follow God in a way that made you seem different than everyone else?** *(Answers will vary, but be prepared to share an experience of your own.)*

○ **Abraham was a man who stood up by himself and went to God on behalf of his people. How do you think he felt?** *(Abraham might have felt overwhelmed or scared for Lot and his family.)*

○ **Is it okay to feel scared when God asks us to stand up and do something no one else is doing?** *(Allow students to explore this idea. God can give us courage when we're afraid, He calls us to be strong and courageous, we can trust God to be near us and watch over us when we stand for Him.)*

○ **What can we do to stay strong when we're alone in doing the right thing?** *(Listen to kids' suggestions. We can pray for strength, remember God's promises, ask for help from other strong friends and adults, etc.)*

WE ALL LIVE IN A YELLOW SUBMARINE

A problem-solving activity uses the Bible to find answers.

Bible Basis:
Genesis 24

Memory Verse:
Guide me in your truth and teach me, for you are God my Savior, and my hope is in you all day long.
Psalm 25:5

BIBLE BACKGROUND

Who doesn't love a good romantic story with a happy ending? A promise, a guiding sign, a loyal love, and a blessing are all a part of the wonderful story of Isaac finding his wife Rebekah.

Abraham, confident of God's promise of many offspring, trusted his servant to go and find a wife for his son Isaac. His servant, Eliezer, asked God to give him a special sign to know which was the perfect girl he was to bring back. He asked that Isaac's future wife would offer to draw water for his 10 thirsty camels to drink. Camels drink a great deal, so this was not a small thing to ask! If the girl offered to do this, the servant knew God was guiding him.

Rebekah not only offered water for the camels, but also food and a place to stay for Eliezer. Laban, Rebekah's brother, (who in that society gave the sister in marriage) welcomed him. After hearing Eliezer's testimony of the sign he asked of God, Laban agreed to give Rebekah to Isaac.

God's providence and blessing are always brought about by His guidance in our lives. Are we seeking that guidance wholeheartedly as Abraham, Isaac, Rebekah, and Eliezer did?

TEACHER TIPS

- While students are working through the Instrument Panel Questions using the Bible, you can facilitate in a way that directs, but doesn't give them the answers. Some clues will be easy to figure out and some will take more thought, but this is part of the process.

- Some students may turn this into a race. You can use this opportunity to point out that when we rush to a decision, we may not hear God's direction clearly and may make wrong choices.

- Just as Eliezer was rewarded for looking for God's guidance, you might want to give a prize at the end for students who were faithful to follow God's directions.

SUPPLIES NEEDED

- Bibles (1 for each group)
- Pencils (1 for each group)
- Masking tape

SETUP

○ Divide students into groups of three or four.

○ Use masking tape to make square boxes on the floor that will serve as a submarine for each group.

○ Photocopy one set of Instrument Panel Questions (page 112) for each group.

○ Give every group a set of questions, a pencil, and a Bible.

RULES TO LIVE BY

Discuss these rules before starting. You may want to write them out and post them at the front of the class.

① You must stay in your "submarine" until the simulation is completed.

② Clues from the Bible will be your instrument panel guide. You'll look up the verse and figure out what to do next.

③ Once you've solved the Instrument Panel Questions, you have completed your voyage.

SIMULATION

You're in a dark, enclosed area. At times you feel claustrophobic and afraid. There are strange creatures and adventures right outside your door! Being in a submarine can be exciting and yet a little overwhelming.

You'll check the instrument panel of God's Word while in the submarine to help you make decisions to get you safely to the next destination. At times you may be fooled by what's around you, wanting to go a certain way instead of trusting and following the instrument panel. It's important to follow your instrument panel to guide you in the right direction. Which will you trust— what you see or what the instrument panel tells you?

Once students have finished the simulation, review the following Instrument Panel answers before moving to the discussion questions. Let them know that it's okay if their decisions are slightly different from yours.

① Be on guard! Be alert!

② Enter through the narrow way.

③ Do everything you can to get the pearl.

④ Trust the backup boats; don't shoot back.

⑤ Be filled with the Holy Spirit to receive power.

ANALYZING THE SITUATION

○ **How is this submarine trip a lot like your life?** (*Kids will probably point out that life is full of obstacles and problems that we need to figure out with God's help.*)

○ **Did you ever just feel like figuring out what to do yourself, and not taking the trouble to read the verse?** (*Let kids share their experiences. Some groups might admit to rushing ahead or trying to look at other people's answers.*)

○ **A lot of people make big decisions without ever checking God's Word as their guide. What can happen if we do it this way?** (*we can make foolish decisions, we can be selfish, we might make mistakes and have to learn the hard way, etc.*)

○ **When have you used God's Word to guide you through a tough situation?** (*Some kids may have experiences to share, but be prepared to share a situation in your own life that your students can understand.*)

Ice CREAM— YOU SCREAM!

A role-playing scenario with a peace-making message.

Bible Basis:
Genesis 32:1—33:17

Memory Verse:
If it is possible, as far as it depends on you, live at peace with everyone.
Romans 12:18

BIBLE BACKGROUND

Jacob always wanted what his brother had, and he finally got it—but at a great price. After using deception to get Esau's birthright and blessing, Jacob left for almost 20 years to escape Esau's anger.

While he was living with his uncle Laban, Jacob himself was the victim of trickery when Laban sent him Leah on his wedding night rather than his beloved Rachel. After working additional time to earn the right to marry Rachel, Jacob again was the target of Laban's deception. In return, Jacob turned the tables and manipulated the breeding of sheep to gain more wealth from his uncle.

Despite his success and God's promises to him, Jacob was still afraid of his brother's response to losing his birthright, even after 20 years. In the end, when Jacob took his wives, children, servants, and wealth to return to his homeland, making peace with his brother was foremost on his mind. He gave portions of the blessings he'd received—550 animals in all—to Esau as a gift of reconciliation and to appease what Jacob perceived as his justifiable anger.

Living at peace with others can truly be a challenge at times. It seems that some people do all they can to be difficult. But we can ask the Lord to give us the right attitude as we lay aside our own desires. Living at peace with others brings us to a place of blessing far beyond any material possessions.

Teacher Tips

○ Students will love role-playing a situation that's familiar to them. You won't have to prompt or tell them how to argue over ice cream! Some will have a compassionate heart to do what's right, while others will naturally want to be first or get what they think they deserve.

○ Encourage the boys and girls to go ahead and role-play however they want in this situation. Stop hurtful words and encourage those who are peacemakers. Look for examples of good decision making to bring up during the debriefing time at the end.

○ If you prefer to have the entire class participate, you may duplicate the roles or just give the extra kids various amounts of money to see how they'll respond to the situation.

○ It will work best for the teacher to role-play the part of the ice cream man. You should not mediate, but let the kids work out their problems.

○ If you have the means of providing real ice cream for this simulation, it will enhance the excitement as it's played out. Be sure to check with parents for food allergy concerns ahead of time if you choose this option.

Supplies Needed

○ Play money that includes at least twenty $1.00 bills, at least one $5.00 paper bill, and 20 quarters

○ A large box or table to represent an ice cream truck

○ A sign reading "Ice Cream $2.00"

○ Roles written on slips of paper (1 for each student)

○ Cooler

○ Construction paper and markers for making ice cream wrappers

○ *Optional:* real ice cream treats

Setup

○ Set up your ice cream truck by making ice cream wrappers from construction paper and placing them in a cooler on the table. Or better yet, use a cooler with real ice cream inside.

○ Give each student a role written on a slip of paper. Tell kids not to show their roles to others.

○ Give each student the money indicated for his or her part.

○ You can duplicate roles if needed for a larger class, or split into two groups. Feel free to create other roles as well.

Roles:

Sam has $5.00 he has saved for a long time. He is 11 years old, and just moved into the neighborhood. He is lonely.

Sue has only 50 cents and asks for help often. She is 10 years old.

John, the neighborhood bully, has only a quarter to spend. He is 10 years old and likes to pick on others.

Emily, an eleven-year-old, has two dollars, but she is selfish and doesn't know how to share with others.

Jessica has no money at all. She is 12 years old and often whines when she doesn't get her way.

Riley just turned 12. He has $1.50 and he'll do whatever he can to get some ice cream.

Rules to Live By

Discuss these rules before starting. You may want to write them out and post them at the front of the class.

① Each ice cream costs $2.00.

② All the characters should try to buy ice cream, but they must act within the traits they were given in their roles.

③ You can't discuss your character traits with anyone.

SIMULATION

Hand out the roles to each student participating and give everyone time to read through the slips of paper. Remind them not to share the information with anyone.

Sam just moved into a new neighborhood from outside the country. The moment he hears that beautiful sound of happy music coming from the ice cream truck, he runs outside in anticipation. Ice cream cones, fruit bars, ice cream sandwiches, and more are waiting! The truck pulls up and Sam has his money ready. The cost of each ice cream is $2.00. Suddenly, lots of kids swarm around the truck. How will each one respond?

You'll have 10 minutes to enact this scene together. Does everyone understand his or her character role? Are you ready to go?

After watching the students play out this scene, gather them together to discuss and debrief.

ANALYZING THE SITUATION

○ **What was the hardest thing for you in this simulation?** (*Answers will vary based on the roles they were given.*)

○ **What did you do to get some ice cream?** (*Answers will vary.*)

○ **What did you do to make peace with others?** (*Listen to students share their answers. Some may have given extra money away or split an ice cream in half, etc.*)

○ **Why would making friends with these kids be important to Sam?** (*He's the new kid and would like to have friends in his neighborhood.*)

○ **How can we show others that our relationships with people are more important than having things?** (*we can show our love by sharing what we have, by looking for ways to make peace with others, etc.*)

○ **In the Bible, Jacob did what he could to hopefully be at peace with his brother Esau. Why is peace hard for some people? Has that ever been hard for you in your family?** (*Listen to kids share their answers. Be prepared to give an example from your observations as well.*)

JAIL JURISDICTION

A fun whodunit game based on the story of Joseph and Potiphar.

Bible Basis:
Genesis 39:1—41:57

Memory Verse:
Whatever you do, work at it with all your heart, as working for the Lord, not for men.
Colossians 3:23

BIBLE BACKGROUND

Joseph's life reads like one long soap opera: a favorite son of his father; despised by his brothers; almost murdered; sold into slavery; rising to service in a high-ranking official's house; falsely accused by the official's wife; thrown into prison; seemingly forsaken by those who could rescue him—only to rise at the end to a place ranking second to Pharaoh himself.

Any one of these circumstances may have overwhelmed an average person. Yet each time, God faithfully brought Joseph through, and each time he was given a place of leadership after incredible suffering. Wherever Joseph was, whether a slave, in prison, or in command of others, he served God wholeheartedly.

God honored Joseph's faithfulness. During a time of famine and hardship, Joseph was given charge over the storehouses throughout Egypt. Joseph used both humility and power for the glory of God. He kept his sights on a faithful Father who turned harm into good, tragedy into blessing, and false accusation into honor.

Wherever God places us, whether in humble circumstances or places of power, we can know that our faithful God will bring us safely through. Encourage your students today that God can and does use every circumstance in our lives.

Teacher Tips

○ For this game you'll need to create your own cards to represent the characters in the Joseph story. The object will be to find out "who did it." Players will try to discover, trick, or convince depending on what character they're playing.

○ It's very important to practice playing this before you begin. It will take tweens one or two practice runs to fully understand what they are to do. Once students get the hang of this game, they won't want to stop!

○ Be sure to act as the narrator so they observe a correct modeling of that role. Following the narrator script closely will be vital to the flow and understanding of the game.

○ Be sure to have the room set up with a table (or tables) and chairs. If you have a small class, you may all play together. If you have a larger class, you can divide into two or more groups with a leader in each group to play the narrator. Each group will have its own simultaneous game.

○ It's best to use a pencil when making your character cards so that the symbols won't show through the cards and give away any clues. Also, instruct the players not to peek at each other's cards, as this would ruin the game.

Supplies Needed

○ Colored index cards

○ Pencil

○ The following cards per group:

Jailer Card: a square with vertical bars to look like a jail
Pharaoh Card: a crown
Potiphar and his wife: two cards with a cloak on each
Joseph cards: blank, enough for remaining students in each group

Setup

○ Make enough cards—so each student can have one—by adding as many blank (Joseph) cards as you need. Hand out all the cards. Tell students to secretly look at their cards to learn what their role is. They are not to share their role with anyone.

○ Be aware that the object of this game is to find out which two players are Potiphar and his wife. Meanwhile, these two characters are trying to put everyone else in jail.

RULES TO LIVE BY

Explain these rules and roles before starting. You may want to write them out and post them.

① Each symbol represents a specific role in the game.

② Participants are to keep their roles secret.

③ Your goal is to find out which players are Potiphar and his wife.

Narrator: The teacher or another leader, who conducts the simulation and and tells when someone correctly identifies Potiphar and his wife.

Jailer: One card. Symbol is a square with vertical bars. The jailer is like a police officer trying to find who is wrongly throwing people in jail.

Pharaoh: One Card. Symbol is a crown. After the first round, Pharaoh can realease one person per round from jail, including himself.

Joseph: Multiple cards—as many as needed to complete the number of students. The Joseph cards remain blank. Anyone who is not one of the other three characters is an innocent "Joseph."

Potiphar and his Wife: Two cards: Symbol is a cloak. Boys or girls can receive these cards. Potiphar and his wife are trying to throw all the innocent Josephs in jail without being discovered for who they are.

SIMULATION SCRIPT

Potiphar's wife falsely accused Joseph of a horrible crime and got him thrown into jail!

You're a humble jailer who realizes Joseph is innocent and wants to get to the bottom of this injustice. You want to help Joseph by bringing the culprits to light. A little detective work is needed. You'll investigate this case. You must find out who Potiphar and his wife are. It's late at night. Everyone close your eyes and lay your heads on the table.

Whoever is holding the cards for Potiphar and his wife, please lift your heads and open your eyes. Choose one player to put in jail by quietly pointing to him or her. Then put your heads down and close your eyes. Announce out loud who has been sent to jail. That person will stay in jail throughout play unless released or Potiphar and his wife are found.

Whoever is holding the Jailer card, please lift your head and open your eyes. You're trying to discover who Potiphar and his wife are. Point secretly to any person, and I'll nod if it's one of them or shake my head if it's an innocent Joseph. Then put your head down and close your eyes.

Only after the first round, allow Pharaoh to release one person from jail. **If you're holding a Pharaoh card, lift your head and point to someone you would like to save from jail. Pharaohs can also save themselves from jail. Pharaoh put** your head down and close your eyes.

After every round, including the first, complete the game by guessing who are Potiphar and his wife. **Everyone open your eyes and lift up your heads. Without revealing your secret identities, discuss who you think Potiphar and his wife are and give reasons why.** (For example, someone might look guilty, have a smile that gives his or her identity away, was heard moving, etc.) **Jailer, you may not reveal that you are the jailer and know the answer, but you can try to convince people to vote correctly through any other evidence you've uncovered.**

Any player may start accusing anyone who they think might be Potiphar or his wife. When an accusation has been made, all the players vote guilty or innocent (including the accused). If the accused are voted innocent, another accusation is made until two players are found guilty. If an innocent player is voted guilty, he goes to jail, but announces his innocence. If an accused player actually is guilty, announce the correct conviction. Only one guilty party may be uncovered in a given round, so play continues until both Potiphar and his wife are found.

ANALYZING THE SITUATION

○ **What made you trust or not trust others in the group?** *(Some students may admit it was hard to tell; others may point to body language or actions.)*

○ **Potiphar and his wife, how did you act to appear innocent when you knew you were guilty?** *(Let students share their strategies.)*

○ **Pharaoh and the Jailer, how did you decide whom to investigate or save?** *(Answers will vary.)*

○ **Innocent Josephs, how did you feel if you got put in jail?** *(Answers will vary.)*

○ **When was it hard to have a good attitude while playing the game?** *(Most students will feel that being wrongly accused makes having a good attitude hard.)*

○ **How did Joseph react to his circumstances when he was wrongly accused?** *(Joseph was able to trust God since he knew he was innocent.)*

○ **Everyone will be treated unfairly at some time in his or her life. How can we be faithful to God when things aren't fair?** *(Answers will vary. Point out that we can't always make it right; sometimes we have to let God take care of it.)*

RESPONSIBILITY ROCKS

A family scenario illustrates the differences between human weakness and divine perfection.

BIBLE BACKGROUND

Growing up with Jesus as a member of the family must have been quite an experience. We know that Jesus had four half-brothers and several half-sisters (Matt. 13:55–56) so the home He grew up in was no doubt busy and provided a typical Jewish upbringing. In Luke 2:40–52, we can see that Jesus' childhood included normal growth physically, mentally, and socially.

Most Jewish families attended three major festivals in Jerusalem every year. These included Passover, the Feast of Weeks, and the Feast of Tabernacles. Though travel was quite a hardship for many, efforts were especially made to go to Jerusalem for the Passover. This time was set aside for a solemn festival, but it was also celebrated as a grand holiday. Large groups of extended family usually traveled together for safety reasons as well as for the fellowship.

As your tweens consider what it would be like growing up with Jesus, help them understand that Jesus was once the same age as they are now. Jesus' divine perfection allowed Him to model the kind of responsibility to which young people should strive.

TEACHER TIPS

○ Your careful observation during the simulation will help you identify points of interest to use during your post-activity discussion. Look for contrasts between the selfless point of view of the Jesus character and the potentially more self-serving actions of the other siblings.

○ Be sure to emphasize the importance of secrecy for this game. Let students know that if they suspect one of their siblings is playing the role of Jesus, they should keep it to themselves until the discussion time.

SUPPLIES NEEDED

○ Slips of paper in a bowl or hat (see Setup)
○ Poster board or whiteboard and marker

SETUP

○ Write "Jesus" on several slips of paper so you'll have one for all groups but one. Write "sibling" on the remaining slips, having enough for one per student.

○ Choose one group ahead of time who will not have a Jesus character, but don't tell the group. They'll function as a contrast to the other groups.

○ Divide kids into groups of three or four and have each person draw slips for their roles. (They must absolutely keep their identities secret.)

Post these scenarios:

① Your best friend's dog ran away this morning.

② You've been invited to a birthday party tonight, but you don't have a gift yet.

③ Your Grandma is sick in the hospital.

④ You have a big test coming up at the end of the week.

⑤ Some friends are going to the beach.

Rules to Live By

Discuss these rules before starting. You may want to write them out and post them at the front of the class.

① You must keep your identity secret, especially if you're "Jesus."

② Your family group must make a unanimous decision about what you'll do.

Simulation

We always picture Jesus as an adult, but when Jesus was a boy, He had the same trials and troubles as every normal kid. The Bible tells us that He was completely human. He fell down, had to do chores, made friends, and was expected to obey His parents. The only difference was He was perfect!

Can you imagine what it would have been like to have a perfect friend or sibling? It's hard to imagine going through childhood with someone who always says the right things, thinks the right thoughts, and obeys every time he or she is asked. What would a day with a perfect kid be like?

Imagine that as a special reward for hard work in school, your teacher gives you the afternoon off. Your group is a family, and you MUST choose how you'll respond together to one of the five scenarios during your afternoon off school. The person who is playing the part of Jesus must try to think like Jesus would and react as He would by putting aside any selfishness or wrong motives.

These are the scenarios you must choose from to decide what your family will encounter for the afternoon. All these situations are happening at the same time, so your family group must choose only one situation.

① Your best friend's dog ran away this morning.

② You've been invited to a birthday party tonight, but you don't have a gift yet.

③ Your grandma is sick in the hospital.

④ You have a big test coming up at the end of the week.

⑤ Some friends are going to the beach.

You have 10 minutes to decide as a group what your family will do for the afternoon, and how each one of you will react to the situation you select. After you decide, be ready to share your decision with the class.

After 10 minutes, each group will share its choice and corresponding response with the rest of the class.

ANALYZING THE SITUATION

○ **Did you make choices differently knowing Jesus was in the group with you?** *(Listen to students' answers.)*

○ **Which group had no Jesus character in their group? Did you figure it out right away, or was it hard to tell? How did you know?** *(Prompt students to be specific about their observations.)*

○ **What was the hardest thing about making your decisions?** *(Most students will identify the struggle to choose between fun things and responsible things.)*

○ **Was it easy to discern which one was Jesus? How?** *(Answers will vary.)*

○ **Will we be able to make perfect choices every time, like Jesus did? Why not? Does that give us an excuse to make bad choices?** *(Listen to students' ideas.)*

TRASH TO TREASURE

A creative activity transforms ordinary trash into something beautiful.

Bible Basis:
2 Chronicles 29:1–19;
John 4:21, 24

Memory Verse:
Let us be thankful, and so worship God acceptably with reverence and awe.
Hebrews 12:28

BIBLE BACKGROUND

King Hezekiah was a man of action. He took the throne at age 25 and ruled for 29 years. His heart was broken by the state in which his father left the temple. This deserted and desecrated place was the one Solomon built in splendor.

Hezekiah was a godly king who followed in the footsteps of King David rather than his evil father, King Ahaz. It took only one month after he became king for him to reopen and repair the temple doors that his father had closed and neglected.

He called on the priests and Levites to cleanse themselves and then work on the temple repairs. After their rededication, they removed all traces of idol worship from the temple and its surroundings, cleaned, and made repairs. It took the priests and Levites 16 days to cleanse the temple, restoring it to its rightful glory and undoing the damage Ahaz caused. Hezekiah wanted the temple to be a place where all could come and worship God freely again.

Today, God calls *us* His temple. First Corinthians 3:16–17 says, "Don't you know that you yourselves are God's temple and that God's Spirit lives in you? If anyone destroys God's temple, God will destroy him; for God's temple is sacred, and you are that temple." As you read this passage today with your class, remind them that God desires them to be cleansed and set apart for His use in the same way that Hezekiah had the temple cleansed and readied for God's use.

Teacher Tips

○ Be sure the trash items you use for this activity are thoroughly clean so you don't end up with a sticky mess.

○ Give students a variety of trash to work with, but limit their time to three minutes.

Supplies Needed

○ Small trash bags or plastic grocery sacks

○ *Clean* trash items to fill one bag for each student (egg cartons, empty yogurt containers, empty soda cans or plastic bottles, balled up newspaper, etc.)

○ Tape, string, and fine-gauge wire

SETUP

○ Set out the string, tape, and wire for students to use as they create their objects.

○ Fill a trash or grocery sack with a variety of trash for each student.

○ Choose a good-natured student to be the designated "trash receiver," but don't tell that person ahead of time.

○ Choose another person who will be a secret "trash collector." He or she will wait for a hidden cue, such as a nose scratch or special phrase that you will give at the right time.

RULES TO LIVE BY

Discuss these rules before starting. You may want to write them out and post them at the front of the class.

① You must try to make something beautiful out of your garbage.

② You must do it within the time limit given.

③ You may not talk with anyone else about what you'll make—it must be your own creation.

SIMULATION

In today's Bible story, Hezekiah had the priests clean out the temple. However, we're going to do something a little different with our trash. We're going to try to turn our trash to treasure. Each of you will be given a bag full of trash. You'll have a short time to create an object that's beautiful. You can transform your materials into a useful object or just something more beautiful than what you started with. Tape, string, and wire are available for you to use as you create.

Any questions? Ready, set, go!

Give students up to three minutes to open their bags of trash and fashion something new.

Okay, everyone stop. Each of you should now take all the trash you don't want to use and throw it out of the bag at the feet of (designate "trash receiver"). The student selected should now be inundated with trash. **Now continue working with what you have left.**

Secretly cue the trash collector to begin picking up garbage and throwing it away as a gesture of kindness toward the person who was "trashed." See if any other students begin to pick up trash rather than continuing to do their own projects.

At this point, end the simulation and lead students in the following discussion.

ANALYZING THE SITUATION

○ **Did you think it was fun to recycle, making something new out of garbage?** (*Answers will vary.*)

○ **Ask the student who was inundated with trash: What did you think when everyone dumped their trash on you?** (*some students will find it made them feel special, others might think it was unfair, etc.*)

○ **What did you think when our trash collector started picking up the extra garbage?** (*The kids who have an eye for injustice might have thought he was trying to gather building materials that weren't his to use. Others might have noticed that he was showing kindness.*)

○ **Hezekiah was a godly man who wanted to cleanse the temple of all the garbage and return the temple to something beautiful for God. Since we're called God's *temples,* what kind of garbage can we clean out of our lives?** (*Encourage kids to be specific about the type of sin or bad behavior they could clean up.*)

BRICKS AND MORTAR

A lively reenactment shows how difficulties can lead to celebration when God intervenes.

Bible Basis:
2 Chronicles 30:1–27

Memory Verse:
Ascribe to the LORD the glory due his name. Bring an offering and come before him; worship the LORD in the splendor of his holiness. *1 Chronicles 16:29*

BIBLE BACKGROUND

The invitations were sent, food preparations were being made, and plans for a celebration were underway. God's people were preparing to observe the celebration marking their escape from slavery in Egypt thanks to the miraculous power of God.

Hezekiah wanted to celebrate the Passover as a sign of repentance and genuine obedience to God. Just as God's angel of death had passed over the doors of the Israelites long before, Hezekiah was seeking God's mercy for his own people. Hezekiah prayed that his people would have sincere hearts toward God, rather than just going through the motions.

In response to the sincere worship, God showed favor to Hezekiah and answered his prayer for healing of the people. The people were so moved to worship during this time that they chose to continue the celebration for a second week!

Setting time aside to bring glory to God's name and seek repentance brings joy and favor in God's sight.

TEACHER TIPS

○ Today's story centers around Passover and Hezekiah's desire that the Israelites celebrate it once again. This activity is an action-packed simulation of the Israelites' slavery in Egypt, from which they were at last delivered by God. As they do so, they'll get an idea of what Passover meant to the Israelites—a time when they remembered, with thankfulness to and humility before God, the very difficult situation from which they had been rescued. The simulation can get a little wild and noisy, but the kids will love it! Students will build a "pyramid" out of "bricks" (newspaper-stuffed paper bags).

○ As students work, your job is to act as the "Pharoah" and do things to discourage them such as knocking bricks off the pile or saying, "You're not working hard enough, go faster!" or "This isn't quality work!" to the point when students begin feeling discouraged or may even want to quit.

○ Give students a short time to finish, such as 10 minutes, which will also create hardship.

○ At the point of complete frustration, stop and begin the debriefing questions.

○ Make note of the kids with good attitudes.

SUPPLIES NEEDED

○ 100 small brown paper bags
○ Several stacks of newspapers
○ Masking tape
○ String

SETUP

○ The goal of this simulation is for students to act as Israelites and build a pyramid at least three feet high. They will do this using bricks they make by stuffing bags with newspaper and closing each bag with string. Initially, you'll supply the materials. Once the simulation starts, play the part of Pharaoh, discouraging them and taking away their supplies one by one.

○ Divide kids into two groups to act as an assembly line. One group will stuff the bags, tie them closed, and then run them to the builders. The second group will build the pyramid in a designated area, using tape to keep the bricks together.

○ Set the bags, string, and newspaper on one table opposite the building site. Set the tape (to be used as mortar) by the designated building site.

RULES TO LIVE BY

Discuss these rules before starting. You may want to write them out and post them at the front of the class.

① Pyramid builders may not talk to each other, but may communicate or encourage others in nonverbal ways.

② You must keep on task at all times.

③ Whatever Pharaoh says, you must do.

④ You must complete the pyramid in the time given.

SIMULATION

You're Israelite slaves living in Egypt. You stamp mud to make bricks in the hot sun all day for the Pharaoh. God communicates through Moses that you'll soon be free and He will lead you out of Egypt!

I am Pharaoh. Make me a pyramid at least three feet high. I have given you what's needed to build. Go to work. Give them about 10 minutes to make bricks to build a pyramid.

After just a minute or so, begin to try to discourage the builders. **You're wasting precious mortar!** Take away the tape. **You must find your own way to keep the bricks together.** Knock down several bricks and tell them to start over.

Go to the brick makers and say, **You're working too slowly. You must find your own brick supplies!** Take away the bags.

The idea is to keep them working in difficult enough circumstances to cause irritation and maybe provoke some bad attitudes.

ANALYZING THE SITUATION

○ **Why was Pharaoh difficult to work for?** *(He was cruel and unfair.)*

○ **How did you respond to hardship while you worked?** *(I complained, I ignored him and did what I wanted, it made me work harder, etc.)*

○ **How did you feel when the activity ended?** *(I was relieved, happy, etc.)*

○ **Why do you think being free of their no-win situation gave the Israelites good reasons to celebrate, even many years later in Hezekiah's time?** *(Answers will vary.)*

○ **Have you ever praised and worshiped God in the middle of a hard time?** *(Allow students to share answers.)* **How does that compare with our ability to worship God when the difficulties are over and we've seen how God's helped us through it?** *(Students may observe that it's easier to celebrate after the fact than in the middle of hard times. Others may say that we depend on God more when the going gets tough. Be prepared to share an example from your life experience.)*

WHO AM I?

A guessing game exposes the truth about Jesus Christ.

Bible Basis:
Isaiah 53:5–6; Matthew 16:13–16; 1 John 4:14–15

Memory Verse:
If anyone acknowledges that Jesus is the Son of God, God lives in him and he in God.
1 John 4:15

BIBLE BACKGROUND

Roughly 700 years before Jesus' birth, God foretold many details of His coming through the prophet Isaiah. Isaiah told us that Jesus would be despised and rejected, and that He would be wounded and crushed for our sin (Isa. 53:5–6).

While Isaiah and other prophets faithfully portrayed God's message, the people continued to turn their backs and close their ears. Many of the prophets were mocked, despised, imprisoned, and killed. Even when the people seemed to listen at first, they often forgot about God's message before long.

Discerning the truth can be hard to do at times. Even with the many prophesies foretelling the Messiah, Jesus' own disciples at first doubted and turned away when He was convicted and crucified.

Today we must all face the same question that Jesus posed to His disciples: Who do you say that I am?

Teacher Tips

- Before starting, provide model questions that will help detect the "real" Jesus, such as: "Where did you come from?" "What do you do for a living?" "What is most important to you?"

- Remind students to stick to their roles. They shouldn't intentionally trick or confuse others. (The only character who is allowed to do this is Judas, but students will not know ahead of time that he's circulating.) You may want to play one of the characters to join in this simulation with your students.

- If you have a large group, you may add characters or use some roles twice.

- Once a student discovers who Jesus is, he or she should not give away the discovery to anyone else. Remind all to act naturally until the activity is finished.

Supplies

- A bag or hat to hold names

- Slips of paper with the following names written on them: Zacchaeus, shepherd boy, John the Baptist, paralyzed man, Peter the disciple, Pilate the Governor, a Pharisee, Martha, Doubting Thomas, servant girl, servant boy, a king, Lazarus, Jesus, temple priest

- One slip of paper should read: *Judas—you may choose to mislead others with your answers.*

- *Optional:* Bible-time costume for each student/role

SETUP

○ Prepare the slips of paper with roles and place in a hat or bag.

○ Each student is to draw a name of a Bible character who would have lived during Jesus' day. (Inform kids that they may not tell anyone which role they picked.)

RULES TO LIVE BY

Discuss these rules before starting. You may want to write them out and post them at the front of the class.

① You must stay in character portraying the person you have chosen.

② You are not allowed to ask directly, "Are you Jesus?"

③ Once you've figured out who Jesus is, don't announce it to anyone else.

SIMULATION

Living in Jesus' day would have been very exciting. Some of your friends may have realized Jesus' true identity. As the Son of God, He could heal, forgive, and had wisdom to solve any problem. But some people didn't recognize or choose to believe that He is truly the Son of God.

In this activity, you want to find Jesus to ask Him questions and get to know Him. You've never seen Him in person; you've only heard about Him from others. Searching to find Him, you ask questions and try to locate this Savior.

We'll all spend 10 minutes wandering about Galilee asking each other questions about our identities. You may only ask one question at a time before turning to another person. When we're finished, we'll see how many people we have identified—and especially, we'll see who found the one playing Jesus!

Does anyone have any questions?

Let's go to Galilee!

ANALYZING THE SITUATION

○ **Who was playing the role of Jesus? What kind of questions did you ask and how did you first recognize him?** *(Allow students to respond.)*

○ **Who were some of the other characters?** *(Give students time to enjoy guessing each other's identities.)*

○ **Who had the part of Judas? How did you try to trick people?** *(Allow your Judas character to share his deceptive answers.)*

○ **Even when Jesus lived, people asked questions and tried to figure out who He really was. How do you think He might have been misunderstood by people?** *(Some of the people thought He was a magician, others thought He was only a good teacher, some thought He was trying to overturn the government, etc.)*

○ **We tried to figure out who Jesus was by asking questions. Even today, some people claim to know who the real Jesus is, but they don't know Him at all. Some false religions try to reshape Jesus into a different person from the One the Bible describes. What things are definitely true about Jesus— things that make Him unique from everyone else?** *(Take a few minutes to discuss the non-negotiable things about Jesus Christ, such as His divine nature, moral perfection, and His sacrifice for us that leads to salvation.)*

TIME WARP!

A time machine drama applies Scripture to solve problems.

Bible Basis:
Jeremiah 36

Memory Verse:
All your words are true; all your righteous laws are eternal.
Psalm 119:160

BIBLE BACKGROUND

God gave Jeremiah a tough job. He was told to write on a scroll all the prophecies God gave him so they could be read aloud to the people. The people were supposed to hear this and turn from their sins. If the people heard and asked for forgiveness, God would forgive them.

Jeremiah shared what God told him no matter how the people responded. He came under opposition from those who wanted to ignore God's Word. King Jehoiakim even cut full columns of the words from the scroll and burned them after they were read to him! At God's command, Jeremiah rewrote the scroll knowing that man could not stop God's Word from going out.

God's Word still goes out today despite fierce opposition from God's enemies. Its message is read, preached, memorized, and shared in hundreds of languages all around the world. The message hasn't changed and never will. It still convicts, heals, challenges, and changes lives just as it did thousands of years ago.

TEACHER TIPS

○ This activity uses mock time-travel to get kids thinking critically while they're practicing biblical application. Be energetic and share your enthusiasm for God's Word.

○ Students may use the concordance found at the back of some Bibles to locate Scripture. While the verses will be listed on a large piece of paper or poster for reference, the challenge is finding a verse that applies well to each situation.

○ Some verses will work for more than one situation, so there may be more than one way to apply a verse. Be flexible and understand your students' thinking process before correcting.

SUPPLIES NEEDED

○ Six Bibles (1 for each group)

○ Index cards

○ List the following Scripture references on a poster board or large piece of paper:

> Isaiah 40:29
> Matthew 7:12
> John 14:27
> Romans 8:28–29
> Romans 10:9
> Romans 12:18
> Philippians 1:6
> James 4:1–2
> 1 Peter 5:10

SETUP

○ Write out or copy the six situations listed below on index cards.

○ Form up to six groups of students. Assign one situation per group.

RULES TO LIVE BY

Discuss these rules before starting. You may want to write them out and post them at the front of the class.

① Every group will go back in history in a time machine.

② You'll be given one "Time Warp" scene (either invented or taken from Scripture) and a Bible to accomplish your task.

③ You must act out your scene in a skit, using Scriptures on the board and others you find to assist you.

④ You may not go forward into the present until you have acted out your scene to the class.

TIME WARP SCENES

Situation #1—Noah is trying to convince people that a flood is coming. He's very discouraged because no one believes him! One person plays Noah while the rest in your group are either mockers or encouragers. The encouragers will need to find Scripture to encourage Noah to keep doing what God told him to do.

Situation #2—Joseph's brothers are ready to throw him in a pit and leave him for dead because of their jealousy. One performer plays the role of Joseph, while the rest play the brothers plotting to throw him in the pit. How does Scripture help the brothers see what they're doing is wrong and encourage Joseph?

Situation #3—You meet a family from the 1930s Depression who is very poor and unable to find work. Your own family doesn't have much either, and you're all suffering. Choose your own acting roles for your presentation. What can you do to help the other family, and how can you encourage them through God's Word?

 Situation #4— Peter and the other disciples are in a fishing boat when a storm hits. The actor who plays Peter sees Jesus on the water, but everyone is terrified. What will you find in the Bible that will help Peter and his friends?

Situation #5— The apostle Paul is in a dark, cold prison, lonely and eager to continue sharing the Gospel with the world. One student plays the part of Paul, and the other actors divide into jailer and fellow prisoners. What will you do to encourage Paul and lead the jail keeper to Christ?

Situation #6—You meet some friends in the lunchroom at school on a Friday in the current year. They're arguing and not getting along.

They don't know Jesus at all. Choose one of you to play the role of a new student, and the rest of the group can act out the kids in the lunchroom. What Bible passage might help introduce them to Jesus?

SIMULATION

Are you ready for a little excitement? Strap on your seatbelts!

You woke up this morning thinking it was a normal Sunday in your modern neighborhood. You and your family are humming along nicely in your car on the way to church when you notice a strange object in the bushes.

Where a telephone pole used to stand, there now sits a machine that looks like a large capsule. Your dad pulls to the side of the road and you get out to investigate. When you open a door on the capsule, a bright light flashes and suddenly you're transported in time and space.

Each of you has a Bible in your hand with Psalm 119:89–91 written on the outside. It includes a note telling you to use God's Word to help out in whatever situation you might face. What are you going to do?

If you ever want to re-enter the present and return to your family, you must accomplish your task. Each group will be given a situation. Some of these come straight from history and others are made-up. Either way, you'll need to act out a short skit using the Scriptures on our board and others you find to encourage your characters.

Any questions, time travelers? Let's go!

When your groups have had time to prepare their skits, call each one up in random order to perform.

ANALYZING THE SITUATION

○ **Would anyone here really like to be able to go back in time? Why or why not?** (*Let students share their answers.*)

○ **Does God's Word only apply to certain times in history? Explain your answer.** (*Clearly, the truths in Scripture are universal. Explore how your students understand its truth transcends time and place.*)

○ **Did anyone have trouble finding a Scripture that seemed to fit your situation? Are some of these Bible verses useful in more than one situation?** (*Listen to students' answers, pointing out situations where more than one passage applies.*)

BRIDGING THE GAP

A rescue mission emphasizes our need for prayer.

Bible Basis:
Matthew 6:5–13

Memory Verse:
Pray continually.
1 Thessalonians 5:17

BIBLE BACKGROUND

When Jesus taught the disciples the model for prayer, He demonstrated three main elements: praise, presenting our needs, and confession of sin. He shows us not only a pattern for prayer, but He also establishes the way in which we should approach God.

First we must acknowledge who God is: He is great; King over all; and holy. When we pray, we need to know who we're praying to. Hebrews 11:6 tells us: "And without faith it is impossible to please God, because anyone who comes to him must believe that he exists and that he rewards those who earnestly seek him."

Next, God wants us to come to Him with our needs because He wants a relationship with us. Isaiah 30:18 tells us that God desires to have compassion on us, that He longs to be gracious to us.

Finally, we need to confess the places in which we fall short of all that God has planned for us. Confession doesn't have to mean beating ourselves up for where we missed it. It's simply a turning away from our own ways and acknowledging that His ways are better, even when we don't understand them.

Prayer can change circumstances and can change us. Talking to God and dwelling on His Word draws us into a more intimate relationship with Him. Discussing answered prayer and communication today can help your tweens understand they have a loving Father who knows all their needs.

TeAcHeR TiPS

○ Students will discover the importance of communication while carrying out a simulated rescue. Let them work it out independently.

○ If they break any of the rules, the group must begin again. Even so, encourage them in their attempts to try again.

○ The instructions call for making "bridges" out of masking tape, but you may use real ladders for this simulation if you choose. If time allows, switch roles so others have a chance to be the missionary guide.

SuPPLieS NeeDeD

○ Masking tape
○ Bandana or towel to blindfold the "blind" person

SeTuP

○ Use masking tape to mark out two to four pretend bridges on the floor or carpet. You can connect five squares together in a row to create the look of a ladder lying on the ground.

○ Divide students into groups of three, giving each one in the group a different role: the missionary guide, a blind orphan, or a deaf child. Tell each one privately, so they don't know each other's roles until the simulation begins. Blindfold the orphans in each group.

RULES TO LIVE BY

Discuss these rules before starting. You may want to write them out and post them at the front of the class.

① You can only communicate within the bounds of your role: The blind person can't see and the deaf person can't hear.

② During the simulation, the missionary may never let his or her hands leave the shoulders of the orphans.

③ You may ONLY step on horizontal lines, which represent the sturdy bars of a bridge. If you step in the space or area inside the squares, you will fall into the river below. You must start over if that happens.

SIMULATION

Today, all of you are going to undertake a very dangerous mission. Do you think you can handle it? Some special skills and a lot of prayer will help you make it through.

Point to the students selected to be the guides. **You are missionaries in a dense**

jungle in Brazil. Dangers lurk everywhere. You must rescue two orphan children out of a dangerous situation and bring them to the missionary compound to live in safety.

As you cross the jungle, you come across a deep canyon. The only way to cross is to go over a rickety old bridge with insufficient places to step. It's more than a mile down to a river of piranhas! It's your only chance and you must cross. How can you get these precious orphans over safely? You must try. You know God will help guide you.

If you're the missionary, you'll have to be very careful to communicate in the best way you can to these helpless orphans. But you have more challenges: one of your orphans can't see at all and the other can't hear. The missionary will need to place his or her hands on the shoulders of an orphan in order to better communicate how to get across the bridge. Remember—if one of your feet steps in between the lines, you'll have to start over. Are you ready to try?

This activity should take about 10 minutes. If time allows, the students can take turns being the guide. When everyone has made it across the bridge safely, gather them together for discussion.

ANALYZING THE SITUATION

○ **What was the most frustrating thing about this situation?** *(Students will probably point out the dilemma of communicating with someone who cannot see or hear.)*

○ **What did you need to do to be able to cross safely?** *(listen, stay connected, trust each other, etc.)*

○ **How is a relationship with God a lot like having a guide through life?** *(Let students grapple with this a bit before jumping in. Perhaps they'll point out that God is kind and trustworthy, that He shows us where to step, or that even when we're handicapped, He communicates to us in ways we can understand.)*

○ **Why is prayer so important in our daily lives?** *(Prayer is a lot like communication with a guide—someone who loves us and stays beside us. Prayer helps us stay in communication with God throughout the day.)*

○ **Sometimes it's hard to pray to God when you can't see Him. What are some things you could do to stay in better communication with God?** *(Encourage students to practice talking to God even when it feels strange or silly. Reading the Bible is also a means of communicating with God.)*

GET OUTTA YOUR ZONE!

A missionary outreach stretches kids' comfort levels.

Bible Basis:
Matthew 14:22–33

Memory Verse:
I can do everything through him who gives me strength.
Philippians 4:13

BIBLE BACKGROUND

Peter was stressed out. In fact, all the disciples must have been. Waves were buffeting their little boat and a huge storm was testing their nerves. In the midst of this turmoil, Jesus came.

Peter took courage and stepped out of the boat to walk to Jesus on the water. Then Peter did what many people might do. He got overwhelmed when he looked at the circumstances in which he found himself. The doubt and fear caused him to begin to sink. He cried out to the Lord, and Jesus reached out to save him.

We all can relate to Peter, who started out in courage, but then trusted in his own strength and forgot to keep trusting in Jesus. Doubt, fear, and panic can sabotage our best intentions, but Jesus is always alongside to rescue us from our fears. Kids can identify clearly with Peter's struggles, but remind them that when we feel the most inadequate God's strength is present and gives us what we need to get through.

Teacher Tips

○ Since this activity is designed to create some discomfort, the more dramatic or outgoing students will find it a bit easier to portray their roles. Others may be shy and have a hard time getting started. Either way, encourage everyone to do their best.

○ Students will be divided into two groups: the missionaries and the Quaydobi people. It may help to set them apart by giving one group bandanas, hats, arm bands, etc. to wear during the activity. In this activity, the rules for each group become very important.

○ Teachers should establish the guidelines clearly and enforce them consistently. If only one teacher is conducting this activity, it might help to enlist others to join you for today. As with any activity involving food, make sure you check for food allergies before serving.

Supplies Needed

○ Paper plates
○ Napkins
○ Bibles
○ Slips of paper
○ Pens
○ Hat or bowl for drawing roles

Choose one of the following "recipes" for the Quaydobi people to share. You may create one of your own, but make sure it will represent a different or challenging taste for your group (these will be used in Quaydobi Rule 3 on page 64).

Horseradish and pickles
Cottage cheese, raisins, and prepared blueberry gelatin
Softened cream cheese mixed with salsa or jalapeño jelly

SETUP

○ Prepare your food items ahead of time.

○ Create a slip of paper for each student in your class. Write the Quaydobi rules on half of the papers and the Missionary rules on the other half—so each student has a paper. Place all of them in a hat for students to draw.

○ As students draw a slip of paper, send them to one side of the room or the other to wait for further instructions. They can begin reading through their list of rules until everyone has drawn.

QUAYDOBI RULES

① You speak English but talk very slowly and softly. It's rude to speak loudly.

② A sign of friendship is to raise your right hand and click your tongue once.

③ You give guests a tasty but odd dish as a gesture of friendship. If someone eats this gift, you are friends and will listen. If someone won't eat your gift, then you walk away.

④ When you understand what someone says to you, blink three times.

MISSIONARY RULES

① You must find a way to build a friendship with a Quaydobi person.

② You must show kindness and respect to those who are different from you.

③ You must share the Gospel with one person who understands.

④ When you understand what someone says to you, blink three times.

RULES TO LIVE BY

Discuss these rules before starting. You may want to write them out and post them at the front of the class.

① You must follow the rules given for your role.

② You should not speak loudly.

③ If a teacher corrects you, be respectful and listen.

SIMULATION

If you're like many kids your age, you live in a nice home, have many friends, and enjoy things such as MP3 players, baseball, and fast food. Life is pretty sweet!

But suddenly, everything you know is about to turn upside-down. Your parents tell you that God has given your family an opportunity to minister to a

country in South America called Quaydobi, to share the Gospel. Your parents tell you that if you step out in faith, God will give you the strength to do what He has called you to do.

You panic! The life of a missionary kid can be hard. You don't really want to leave your comfortable life. But you want to do what God asks even though this seems impossible. What a dilemma!

In Quaydobi the people seem strange and the culture is hard to get used to. How can you leave everything comfortable behind and effectively communicate the Gospel to these people who don't speak your language, don't eat the same things, and don't look anything like you?

You must now enter the Quaydobi village based on the roles you randomly selected. Remember to act according to the rules governing your role. Missionaries, your plane has landed, so now your adventure begins!

As the students circulate around the room, observe how they communicate with each other, giving help only when necessary. After about 10 minutes, gather everyone for discussion time.

ANALYZING THE SITUATION

○ (to the missionaries) **What was the hardest thing you had to do to communicate with the Quaydobi people?** *(Listen to some of the challenges they observed.)*

○ (to the Quaydobi) **Did you ever get frustrated with the missionaries? How did they treat you?** *(Listen to their examples.)*

○ **Which role was harder, do you think—being a missionary or being part of the native tribe?** *(Answers will vary.)*

○ **If God called you to be a missionary to another culture, what would be the hardest thing about it? What would be the most exciting thing about it?** *(Allow for students' responses.)*

A KNIGHT'S TALE (WEEK ONE)*

A medieval journey teaches us to press on in our pursuit of God.

Bible Basis:
Matthew 15:21–28; Mark 11:24; John 14:13–14

Memory Verse:
"Therefore I tell you, whatever you ask for in prayer, believe that you have received it, and it will be yours."
Mark 11:24

BIBLE BACKGROUND

The desperate Gentile woman in Matthew 15 was insignificant as far as the Jews were concerned. But she audaciously brought her needs to Jesus. Because of her loud persistence the disciples became irritated and wanted to get rid of her! Jesus saw her faith and had mercy on her. He loved this Gentile woman enough to see past the disciples' irritation, and He responded by healing her daughter.

At times we can relate to this Gentile woman. We too may feel insignificant and overlooked by the world around us. But Jesus is always ready to hear our cries. He is patient and knows our heart. And rather than being irritated by persistence, He actually instructs us to be unwavering and steadfast in prayer (Luke 18:1–8).

How many times have we turned away someone who is pestering us for something, just as the disciples wanted to do with this woman? This lesson has special significance for young people who may feel ready to give up when they're feeling insignificant or needy. The passage teaches us on two different fronts: We are to be patient and compassionate as the giver, and persistent and steady in our pursuit of God.

* *Note:* This longer simulation will be used over two class times.

TEACHER TIPS

○ As an extended lesson, this activity can work well a couple different ways. You can create a two-part lesson, spanning two weeks. You can also use it as an entire morning's lesson rather than simply an application.

○ Students shouldn't feel limited by the instructions on their cards. Encourage them to embellish and expand their character in new ways.

○ Be prepared to assist the flow of the activity by circulating throughout the room. Prompt students with suggestions and reminders along the way.

○ You can expand the roles of the sages and nobles to fit the number of students in your class so everyone can participate.

SUPPLIES NEEDED

○ Two slips of paper with the word "Pass" written on each (for the servant)

○ A cross necklace (for the servant)

○ A plastic sword (for Lancernot)

○ A Bible (for Lancernot)

○ Plastic or construction paper crowns (for the nobles)

○ Towels or robes to use as cloaks (for the sages)

○ Masking tape or duct tape or heavy 30' rope

SETUP

○ Assign your roles:

Lancernot (sword): While trying to get to the castle and become a knight, this character will face many obstacles. In order to proceed, he must receive a pass from the servant.

Servant (cross necklace and passes): The servant will only provide Lancernot a pass if the specific conditions for each challenge are met.

Nobles (crowns): People Lancernot meets on his journey.

Sages (robes): These groups will handle various situations.

○ Ahead of time, copy the role-play directions for each character in Situations 1 and 2 (page 69) ahead of time and give to the students according to their roles (these directions will be kept secret).

○ Create a path with a winding rope on the floor or mark the path with tape. Include areas for the two groups (nobles and sages) to act out their situations.

RULES TO LIVE BY

Discuss these rules before starting. You may want to write them out and post them.

① Lancernot must always carry a Bible. If it's stolen or lost, he must return home.

② In order to continue to the next area, Lancernot must get a pass from the servant of the king who knows the conditions of each challenge.

③ Physical force must never be used to try to convince Lancernot.

④ You must be loyal to your group.

⑤ You must work to achieve the secret goal given to you.

SIMULATION

Today's activity will require you to be smart, careful, and really creative (look around at your students). **I think we've assembled the perfect group for the job.**

We're now entering the medieval period (bring Lancernot forward to face the group). **I'd like to introduce you to Lancernot, who has grown up as a poor pauper in the woods at a place that has frightened people for centuries. But he's very brave indeed.**

He longs to become a knight and help save others, so he sent word to the king telling him about his dream. The king's humble servant (bring the servant forward) **brings a reply, saying that Lancernot must make a treacherous journey to the castle before he can become a knight.**

Listen carefully, Lancernot. Many people will try to deceive you as you travel. The only way you can proceed to the next challenge is if the servant gives you a special pass. If you arrive safely, the king will make you a knight!

I'll give you each a copy of your tasks. Don't show these to anyone else! You'll see your character's name and will have several minutes to figure out what you need to do to complete your portion of the journey. Let's go to it!

SITUATION #1

Situation #1—(Lancernot) You cross a river with sharp rocks in the riverbed. Badly cut and bleeding, you yell out, "Ouch! My foot is cut and I can't go on!" Who will you ask for help? See what happens, but you may NOT pass until your foot is healed.

Situation #1—(Servant) You notice that Lancernot has been hurt and go to his side. You must wait for Lancernot to ask you for help. If he asks you for help say, "You are healed," and give him the first pass. BUT you can only help him if he asks.

Situation #1—(Sages) Your group immediately comes to Lancernot's side when he gets hurt. Try to convince him that you can heal him by asking things like, "Can I wrap your foot?" or "I'll use healing medicine on your leg if you'll let me," etc. Try to keep him from asking the servant for help. How can you get him to trust you?

SITUATION #2

Situation #2—(Lancernot) You pass through a beautiful land. As you wander and explore, the wonder of the land distracts you and you leave the servant behind. After a while you get tired and choose this place to rest. You start to feel bad about leaving the servant behind. Think about it! What might be the right thing to do?

Situation #2—(Nobles) You must find a way to distract Lancernot from the servant. Your group will promise him that if he bows to the nobles, he will own vast riches of the kingdom. Encourage him to stay by saying things such as, "This is the best land," or "You can always do what you want here."

Situation #2—(Servant) Lancernot leaves you behind as he walks around marveling at the beautiful land. You step away from him and look dejected. The only way Lancernot can go ahead is if he returns to find you and asks your forgiveness for leaving you. If he asks for your forgiveness, give him the second pass.

ANALYZING THE SITUATION

○ **What was Lancernot's goal?** *(He was going to the castle to become a knight.)*

○ **Is it more rewarding to reach a hard goal or an easy goal? Why?** *(Allow discussion.)*

○ **What did the nobles and the sages have in common?** *(They tried to distract Lancernot from his real purpose.)*

○ **Has anyone ever tried to distract you from reaching a goal?** *(Listen as kids share their stories.)*

If this ends today's activity, remind your students that doing something valuable takes hard work. God wants us to press forward in pursuit of good things. Tell students that next time, they'll discover what happens to Lancernot on his quest.

A KNIGHT'S TALE (WEEK TWO)*

A medieval journey teaches us to press on in our pursuit of God.

Bible Basis:
Luke 11:1–13; 18:1–8

Memory Verse:
"Ask and it will be given to you; seek and you will find; knock and the door will be opened to you."
Matthew 7:7

BIBLE BACKGROUND

It would have been amazing to have walked and lived with Jesus. He was the ultimate teacher. The disciples could have asked Jesus to teach them many things, such as how to preach or perform miracles, but what they wanted most was to learn how to pray!

Jesus was a great example of someone who constantly prayed. He prayed at His baptism, in the garden, and at His transfiguration. Jesus often prayed alone.

Jesus gave us a pattern of prayer to guide us. We have his model recorded in Luke 11 and Matthew 6. This prayer shows us to address God as our Father, in a familiar tone, and to seek His purpose for our lives. Persistence in communicating with our heavenly Father helps us gain clearer direction and insight into His will. He longs to lead us and nurture us as His children.

Be confident as you bring your tweens' requests to our heavenly Father. As you keep asking for and modeling a life of dependence on God, your students will see a pattern of going to the Father who cares and forgives.

** **Note:** This is the second part of a two-part simulation.*

TEACHER TIPS

○ You'll need to gather three small items in advance. During one scene, the woodsmen will post a **sign** with an arrow pointing the wrong way in an attempt to trick Lancernot. You can make this easily on any piece of paper. You'll also need a **kingdom map** for the servant and a **blanket** for the sages.

○ As this is a continuation of day one, you'll be able to distribute props and roles more quickly than before. If you've returned after an absence, review the rules and concept so that new students will understand Lancernot's mission. Be sure to introduce the new characters, the woodsmen. These are forest bandits that attempt to cause trouble for Lancernot.

SUPPLIES NEEDED

○ Three slips of paper with the word "Pass" written on each (for the Servant)

○ A cross necklace (for the servant)

○ A kingdom map (for the servant)

○ A plastic sword (for Lancernot)

○ A Bible (for Lancernot)

○ Sticks (for the woodsmen)

○ Sign as described in Teacher Tips (for the woodsmen)

○ Towels or robes to use as cloaks (for the sages)

○ Blanket (for the sages)

○ Masking tape or duct tape or heavy 30' rope

SETUP

○ Assign roles. If possible, have the same students as last week play the parts of Lancernot and the servant.

○ Ahead of time, copy the secret directions for characters in Situations 3, 4, and 5.

○ Create a path with a winding rope on the floor or mark a path with tape. Include areas for the two groups (nobles and woodsmen) to act out their situations.

RULES TO LIVE BY

Use the same rules as used in A Knight's Tale (Week One). See page 68.

Copy the directions below and give them to each person or group in bold letters. Remind students that these are to remain a secret from other characters.

SITUATION #3

Situation #3—(Lancernot) Still journeying, you move off the trail and discover that you are totally lost. You try to consult a compass and scan the horizon, but you don't know where you are. You're getting colder and begin to fear for your safety. Your only hope is to find someone who can tell you the right direction.

Situation #3—(Woodsmen) From a distance, you notice that Lancernot appears lost. Your group tries to trick him by making animal noises and bird calls. One of you places a sign near the path with an arrow pointing the wrong way.

Situation #3—(Servant) After searching for Lancernot, you notice him cold and shivering away from the trail. Approach him and offer him a map. If he agrees to consult your map, you may give him the pass to the next obstacle.

SITUATION #4

Situation #4—(Lancernot) After overcoming several obstacles, you're really feeling tired. Even though you don't have time to spare, you decide to lie down and sleep instead of pressing on to the kingdom. Lie down beside the path and begin to dream . . . Will anyone be able to wake you? Whom will you trust?

Situation #4—(Sages) You notice that Lancernot has fallen asleep beside the road. You want to make sure that he sleeps instead of reaching the castle before dark. Each of you will find a way to keep Lancernot asleep. Sing a lullaby, cover him with a soft blanket, or stroke his head gently. Soon the servant scares you away!

Situation #4—(Servant) You notice that the sages are trying to keep Lancernot asleep. You watch them for a while, but then chase them off by making noise and frightening them. You go to Lancernot and snap your fingers beside his ears to wake him. If he responds and stands to his feet, give him a pass to the next obstacle.

SITUATION #5

Situation #5—(Lancernot) You journey further along the path. Woodsmen jump out of the woods and take you captive. You fight but can't win. How will you escape?

Situation #5—(Woodsmen) You attack Lancernot and take him captive. Don't be too rough, but he must join you. You can tie his hands gently or make him sit down, but you won't let him go. Soon, you'll notice that the servant arrives to make a deal.

Situation #5—(Servant) You were separated from Lancernot. Then you find him surrounded. You must convince Lancernot to let you exchange your life for his, taking his place in the gang of thieves. If he agrees, you may give him the pass.

Once all the situations have been enacted, announce that Lancernot has passed all that's required to become a knight! The groups will stand on the sides while Lancernot kneels in front of you. Taking his sword, gently tap both of his shoulders and announce, **"I present to you Sir Lancernot, proud Knight of the Kingdom!"**
Gather the props and instruct everyone to sit in a circle for some discussion.

ANALYZING THE SITUATION

(Note: These questions are a continuation of those on page 69.)

○ **Does the servant always seem to have Lancernot's best interests in mind? Is he a good friend? Why?** *(Draw out specific examples of how the servant kept sight of his friend's goal. He always helped Lancernot focus on the right path.)*

○ **Lancernot, did you ever wonder if you should follow the servant—or the people distracting you?** *(Let other students share their observations as well.)*

○ **How does this activity remind us of pursuing God?** *(Sometimes we get pulled off course. People who aren't true friends can move us in another direction.)*

○ **If it takes a lot longer to reach our goals, does that mean God isn't there, encouraging and guiding us?** *(Allow kids to acknowledge that seeking God can be hard; but that doesn't mean God is invisible or absent.)*

WESTWARD HO!

A wagon-trail ride demonstrates how God supplies our physical needs.

Bible Basis:
Mark 1:29–31, 35–38;
Luke 19:1–10

Memory Verse:
My God will meet all your needs according to his glorious riches in Christ Jesus.
Philippians 4:19

BIBLE BACKGROUND

The tax collectors in Jesus' time were despised and feared. They were known for cheating people and growing wealthy from stolen money. The Jews also detested them because tax collectors were agents of the Roman government.

When Jesus approached Zacchaeus, He didn't look at the man as others saw him. He looked deep into Zacchaeus's heart and saw the man's longing for repentance. Zacchaeus offered the words of repentance, and his actions reflected the transformation of his heart.

Jesus was a friend to sinners, and His Word tells us that He came to seek and save the lost. The Lord cared about Zacchaeus's needs despite his rough condition. Young people often mistakenly believe that they have to be entirely good for God to care for them. Zaccheus's story is a stirring model of Christ's love and provision for those from all backgrounds.

TEACHER TIPS

○ This simulation explores the difference between needs and wants, helping students understand the concept of provision in greater depth. It's a great time to discover and answer questions about why God's provision doesn't always look like we expect.

○ This survival simulation allows students to engage in critical thinking. During their westward expedition, you might need to prompt specific questions about their supplies, food, or shelter. (How will you be able to start that fire? What weapons do you need for hunting? etc.)

○ The contrast between the luxuries of modern life and the harsh conditions of the Old West are striking. Look for opportunities to prompt a grateful attitude for God's provision.

○ To add visual interest, see if you can gather pictures of the items on the supply list to supplement the words—or even draw them. Got a bandana at home? Wear it today or bring extras for the kids.

SUPPLIES NEEDED

○ Paper for each group

○ Pencils for each group

○ A large poster with these supplies listed on it: dogs, cows, pigs, horses, cats, chickens, pots and pans, utensils, axes, bows and arrows, saws, hammers, medicine, blankets, flour, sugar, salt, meat, oil, water, yarn, lanterns, spinning wheels, seeds, Bibles, clothes, books, plows, quilts, butter churns, candy sticks, balls, handmade dolls, knives, kettles, candles, pillows, nails, coffee, fruit, spices, beans, rice, tents, washtubs, rope, chain

SETUP

○ Write out your master supply list on a piece of poster board.

○ Place students in family groups of four or five.

RULES TO LIVE BY

Discuss these rules before starting. You may want to write them out and post them at the front of the class.

① Your family's wagon is small, so you're allowed to bring only seven items each.

② You must think of the needs of the family to survive.

③ You may bring three animals per family in addition to your seven supply items.

④ At one point on the journey, you must make a flat boat to cross a river and everything must cross on the boat with you.

SIMULATION

You better turn to someone and say "Howdy, Partner!" 'cause you're going to get mighty close to these folks sitting next to you today. I can't wait to tell you what adventure you've got ahead of you!

But wait. Before you think it's all a barrel of laughs, I also have to tell you that life during the Westward Expansion is tough! Planting gardens, fetching water, hunting food, and just surviving can be difficult. Your dad went west to claim land and has been gone for half a year! He's on his way back to take you to your new home.

Your family needs to pack up your wagon and start the long, 12-week journey through the wilderness to your new home. You've got a big family, and it's a long journey, so you must only take what you'll absolutely need. Your dad also wants you to have some things that you like, but survival is the most important thing.

You need to start to load up the wagon. How do you pick things you need, but also what you want to bring? All right, you've got your family beside you, so let them help you decide. As a family, write a list on your paper of the supplies you'll need. Don't forget the rules, and keep in mind what you'll face on the journey.

Now, get that wagon ready to roll!

ANALYZING THE SITUATION

○ **What did your family choose to bring on the trip, and why?** *(Allow students time to share. Each team will probably present very different ways of approaching the problem. Point out the items teams picked that were the same and the things one team thought of that others missed.)*

○ **Why was it important for you to bring only what you needed on this trip?** *(Most students will observe that when space and expense are limited, we must choose only the necessities to survive.)*

○ **Would you have wanted to live during the 1800s? Why or why not?** *(Listen to students share their answers.)*

○ **Did anyone in your group want to bring something that you thought wasn't that important? What was it? How did you decide what to do?** *(Let students share their compromises.)*

○ **Do you ever think that you have too much stuff at home? If you only had what you needed to survive, what would your bedroom look like?** *(See if kids can visualize the difference between material excess and necessity.)*

○ **If you were moving today, and there was very limited space in the moving van, would you ask your parents to bring things you need or things you want?** *(Answers will vary.)*

○ **The Bible tells us that God meets our needs, but does that mean He gives us all the stuff we want?** (Listen to answers.) **What does the Bible promise about our needs?** *(Refer to Philippians 4:19.)*

BETHLEHEM BARTER

A Holy Land marketplace prompts us to worship Jesus.

Bible Basis:
Luke 2:1–20

Memory Verse:
"Today in the town of David a Savior has been born to you; he is Christ the Lord."
Luke 2:11

BIBLE BACKGROUND

Shepherds in Bible times lived in cold and lonely places caring for stinky sheep. They were considered insignificant in society. Yet God sent His angels out into the fields on a dark night to tell the shepherds of the birth of the Messiah. The most wonderful news ever told was given first to the most ordinary of people.

Hearing the announcement from the angels, the shepherds had to choose whether to believe and act on the news or ignore it and go back to their work. The shepherds chose to wholeheartedly worship and celebrate Jesus' birth.

Just as the shepherds had to choose how they would respond to the good news of Jesus' birth, we also have a choice to make. Do we continue on with our daily lives as though nothing has happened? Or do we take the time to go worship the one born King?

Teacher Tips

○ Make sure you read through the rules carefully before supervising this activity. It may seem chaotic at first, but as the students begin to discuss their options, most will figure out how to accomplish their task.

○ If you don't have bandanas, any colored squares of cloth will work equally well.

○ To add interest, you might want to give the priests real gift boxes and the shepherds stuffed-animal sheep (or a picture of one) to carry around during this activity.

○ Remind students that, according to the Bible, the wise men were the only ones who gave Jesus physical gifts. In the real events that occurred, the shepherds brought the gift of worship. The shepherds in this role-play bring the gift simply for the sake of the activity and the lesson it teaches.

Supplies Needed

○ A copy of each student's role

○ Bowl for kids to draw roles

○ Purple bandanas for priests

○ White bandanas for shepherds

○ Blue bandanas for townspeople

○ Red bandanas for Romans

Setup

○ Make copies of the student roles (three shepherds and equal amounts of priests, townspeople, and Romans).

○ Arrange colored bandanas for each group.

○ Roles:

Shepherds (white bandanas): You're excited about bringing a gift to worship the newly born Messiah, Jesus Christ! But you need some help. All you have is one sheep to trade for a gift. See if you can work it out with someone.

Priests (purple bandanas): The Romans require you to do some work for the census in Bethlehem. You must line up everyone quickly in alphabetical order—by the last letter of their first name, including shepherds and townspeople. If you don't accomplish this, the Romans will punish you. In the meantime, you each have a gift, and the shepherds would love to trade their sheep for what you have. But you can't

trade directly with shepherds; a townsperson will have to come to you as their spokesman.

Townspeople (blue bandanas): The Bethlehem census is bringing your family to town, and you need to find a sheep in order to have enough milk for the crowd of visiting family members. Can you find a shepherd who would be willing to work out a deal with you?

Romans (red bandanas): The census in Bethlehem is a lot of work. Your job is to make sure that the priests are putting everyone in alphabetical order according to the last letter of their first name. If they don't accomplish this by the end of the game, you must punish them by taking their purple bandanas away from them.

RULES TO LIVE BY

Discuss these rules before starting. You may want to write them out and post them at the front of the class.

① Try to stay in character the entire time.

② Make every effort to achieve your character's goal before your teacher ends the activity.

③ Don't get frustrated. Everyone has a different goal.

SIMULATION

I can see today that you're ready to live in Bethlehem, an important city!

As you probably know, the shepherds outside the city weren't the most important people in society. But one night, they got the surprise of their lives! Angels appeared to share the incredible news of Jesus' birth. Now the shepherds wanted to worship Jesus. The present the real shepherds gave Jesus that night was the gift of worship—a great gift, indeed. But today, the shepherds will seek an additional present to give, the kind you can wrap up. Where would the shepherds get presents?

Today you'll spend some time in Bethlehem. Each of you has a special role to play, and it's your job to accomplish your task in the time allowed. When our activity begins, you'll mingle with townspeople, shepherds, priests, and Romans. You'll have to communicate clearly with others to achieve your goal, and it might be harder than you think!

If you accomplish your task before the time is up, go immediately to your teacher. Has everyone read and understood what their role is? Off we go!

As your students mingle throughout the crowd, prompt them to form alliances that will help them reach their goals. Don't help with negotiations and deal-making, but step in if two people have created an impasse.

Provide 10 to 15 minutes for this activity. Anyone who achieves his or her goal sooner will step out of the game. When time is up, begin the discussion.

ANALYZING THE SITUATION

○ **Were you expecting it to be so difficult to get your task done? Why was it harder than you thought?** *(If you're the only one on a mission, then it's easy. But when people have different goals, it takes compromise and patience.)*

○ **Who had the most important task of all?** *(The shepherds had more than just everyday tasks. They wanted to worship to God.)*

○ **What's so cool about the angels telling the lowly shepherds about Jesus' birth? After all, they didn't tell the rulers, priests, and religious leaders first.** *(God singled out outcasts for the hopeful message. His message was for everyone, not just powerful, famous, or important people.)*

○ **Sometimes it's hard to honor God when everyone else has a different purpose. What can we learn from the shepherds?** *(The shepherds were eager to worship Jesus even when it seemed as though they had nothing else to offer. We too can offer ourselves to Christ. Even when it seems we have little to give to God, we can always worship—and that's a gift God loves!)*

I GOTTA HAVE IT!

A "temptation zone" illustrates our need for spiritual defenses.

Bible Basis:
Luke 4:1–13

Memory Verse:
I have hidden your word in my heart that I might not sin against you.
Psalm 119:11

BIBLE BACKGROUND

Times of trial and temptation are never easy, but God offers resources that can help us through them and in the end change us for the better. Using Matthew's account (see Matt. 4:1–11) as the chronological record, we consider that Satan came to Jesus after He had been in the desert fasting and praying for 40 days and nights. Jesus was physically hungry, yet He was so full of the Spirit and well-versed in Scripture that when Satan came, He was ready.

Jesus depended on God and He was obedient to His Word. Hebrews 4:15–16 tells us, "For we do not have a high priest who is unable to sympathize with our weaknesses, but we have one who has been tempted in every way, just as we are—yet was without sin. Let us then approach the throne of grace with confidence, so that we may receive mercy and find grace to help us in our time of need." Jesus was tempted in every way we are, and He can now be a faithful intercessor for us.

To each temptation Satan threw His way, Jesus responded with Scripture. We also can use Scripture when we're tempted. We need to know God's Word, memorize it, and study it so we have a ready answer as Jesus did. And we can count on God to be with us in our temptations, strengthening us and guiding us. One way He may do this is through His Word.

You can help your tweens see that they can face the temptations that come their way with confidence as they rely on God's Word for answers and assurance. "God is our refuge and strength, an ever-present help in trouble" (Ps. 46:1).

Teacher Tips

○ After this exercise is over, you may want to offer to share some of the tempting treats on the table. If so, be sure to check with parents in advance for any food allergies.

Supplies Needed

○ Bandanas or scarves to use for blindfolds

○ Goodies that will tempt students to touch, eat, drink, etc. Ideas follow:

  An ice-cold drink or juice box

  A plate of chocolate candies or candy bars

  A hand-held video game player with a kids' game loaded and ready to play

  A bowl of potato chips or corn chips

  A tray of doughnuts

  A pile of loose change

○ Clean sheet

○ Table

○ Poster board or large sheets of paper (for signs)

○ Markers (for signs)

SETUP

○ Line the longest wall of your classroom with tables that contain items from the list above or other "goodies" that may tempt your students.

○ Cover the table with a clean sheet so no one can see the items until you're ready.

○ Place a sign on the wall or the table that says, "Temptation Zone."

○ Add a sign to the table that says, "Not for you! Keep away."

RULES TO LIVE BY

Discuss these rules before starting. You may want to write them out and post them at the front of the class.

① Once your blindfold is on, you may not remove it until instructed.

② Do not touch anything on the table.

③ Obey the leader's instructions without questions.

SIMULATION

Have you been wondering what's under the cloth covering the table? Well, at last you get to find out!

First, though, put on these blindfolds. Later I'll take the cloth covering away and I'll show you what's there. Have students tie on blindfolds. Let them know when you're removing the cloth. Then one by one, lead them to the table, past it, and back to their seats.

I'm guessing your curiosity still isn't satisfied, is it? Now you can take off your blindfolds and walk past the Temptation Zone. Just remember, those things aren't for you.

Allow students time to file past the table. If anybody tries to take something, remind them that everything is off limits. When everyone has had a good look at the Temptation Zone, gather everyone together for debriefing questions.

ANALYZING THE SITUATION

○ **Did you have any trouble with temptation when you had the blindfold on?** *(Allow students to share answers. Most were probably curious but not tempted when wearing the blindfolds.)*

○ **How did you feel after you saw the goodies on the table?** *(There were things, no doubt, that kids wanted to pick up or have. Let them answer openly.)*

○ **Which things were the most tempting? Why?** *(Answers will vary.)*

○ **The blindfold served as a tool for avoiding the temptation of the items on the table. Blindfolds wouldn't be very helpful in real life, though. God gives us Scripture as a powerful tool for fighting temptation. How can we use this tool?** *(We can be sure we know Scripture well and remember what it says when we're tempted.)*

○ **What kinds of real temptations do we face?** *(Answers will vary.)*

○ **How else does God equip us when those things confront us?** *(His Spirit in us helps us resist temptation, prayer, etc.)*

BIBLE SMUGGLERS

Simulating sending Bibles into foreign countries teaches the reality of global persecution.

Bible Basis:
Luke 24:13–35

Memory Verse:
These are written that you may believe that Jesus is the Christ, the Son of God, and that by believing you may have life in his name.
John 20:31

BIBLE BACKGROUND

Many of us listen to our favorite song over and over until we know the words by heart. In the same way a familiar Bible verse can also bring comfort when it's embedded in our hearts.

The travelers on the road to Emmaus in Luke 24 probably felt weary and discouraged. They had high hopes that Jesus was going to redeem Israel. It was the third day after Jesus' death and now it looked like all their hopes were dashed. It was only when they heard Jesus speaking Scripture to them that their hearts burned within them. Later, when Jesus broke bread with them, they recognized the resurrected Christ. Their hope, strengthened by the Scripture Jesus shared, was not in vain.

In our culture, access to the Word of God is often taken for granted. Consider those with multiple copies of the Bible who never open them! Around the world, many Christians equate the Bible with life and food, and they often have to hide it from oppressive governments or state-run police. Its powerful message of life brings hope.

During this activity, students will be reminded of how valuable this message is to those suffering around the world.

TeACHeR TiPS

○ Bringing Bibles into foreign countries is sometimes a risky and serious endeavor. Your students should understand that Bibles are never to be taken for granted.

○ If you have some particularly rowdy students, place them in less aggressive roles, such as the church leaders.

○ If you don't have enough Bibles available, you can substitute pieces of paper, gospel tracts, or other books. Remind students to show respect for the Bible by not throwing it around or treating it merely as a game prop.

SuPPLieS NeeDeD

○ A large supply of Bibles (small New Testaments work well)

○ Masking tape

SeTuP

○ Use a piece of masking tape to divide the room down the middle. Your line will function as the border of two countries.

○ In one corner tape a large square on the floor or carpet to function as a jail cell.

○ Divide your students into different roles according to the instructions below: two underground church leaders, one jailer, two or more border guards, and two or more Bible smugglers.

Underground Church Leaders: These characters will wait in chairs on one side of the room for the Bible smugglers to bring them as many Bibles as possible. They can try to distract the guards, but they cannot get up out of their seats.

Border Guards: If someone holding a Bible approaches these characters at the border, the border guards must ask the following questions: Who is Jesus? Do you believe in Him? Why is the Bible so important? If the smuggler can answer all three questions, then he's allowed to pass to the other side and give one of the Bibles to the church leaders. If he can't answer questions correctly, the border guard confiscates the Bible and sends the smuggler to the jail for two minutes.

Bible Smugglers: These characters try to get as many Bibles as possible to the church leaders on the other side. If they give a satisfactory answer to the guards, OR if they're able to cross the border while the others are interrogating someone else, they're allowed to give a Bible to a church leader. However, if they sneak past to deliver a Bible, but can't sneak back to the other side without being stopped, they'll have to spend two minutes in jail.

Jailer: The jailer will keep track of the smugglers who end up in jail. The jailer will time each prisoner's two-minute sentence before setting him free.

RULES TO LIVE BY

Discuss these rules before starting. You may want to write them out and post them at the front of the class.

① If you're stopped at the border by a guard, you must listen to his questions and answer them completely and as honestly as possible.

② If you're sent to jail, you must stay there for two minutes before you're released.

③ Church leaders can't get out of their chairs.

④ You must never toss or throw a Bible to someone during this activity. Always hand it gently.

SIMULATION

How many of you own a Bible at home? Do some of you have more than one? Have you ever worried that owning or reading a Bible could get you thrown in jail or arrested? Probably not!

But in many countries around the world, governments don't allow their people to read and study God's Word. Imagine you're in a foreign country that has forbidden the sharing of the good news of Jesus Christ. A group of you is trying to take Bibles across the border and give them to underground church leaders. People are counting on you to help them!

Rumors have indicated that it's not easy to get past the border patrol. One wrong move and you could be sent to prison. Will you be able to complete your mission?

Take time to explain to each group the parameters of their roles as border guards, Bible smugglers, church leaders, or jailers. Let the students begin the activity, giving them time to complete their mission. When they finish, let the church leaders announce how many Bibles they'll be able to distribute to their church members.

ANALYZING THE SITUATION

○ Even during Jesus' day, the Scriptures brought comfort to Christ's followers. Why do you think it's important to memorize verses today? Is it just to impress your parents or Sunday school teachers? *(Help your students recognize the spiritual impact of meditating on Scripture to bury it deep in their hearts. It isn't merely a check-off box of good things to do.)*

○ Did anyone end up going to jail? Imagine if this were real! How did this activity help you understand better what people around the world endure just to read a Bible? *(Listen to answers.)*

○ How did you answer the border guards' three questions? Was it hard to answer, or did you know what to say right away? *(Listen to students share their answers.)*

CAN YOU HEAR ME NOW?

A family communication exercise helps us understand God's love for His children.

Bible Basis:
John 3:1–16

Memory Verse:
Everyone who believes in him may have eternal life.
John 3:15

BIBLE BACKGROUND

Many people go about their day-to-day lives thinking they're pretty good people. They believe that as long as they don't do anything really "bad," God will let them enter heaven when they die.

God's heart longs for a personal relationship with us, but He is a holy God, set apart from any type of sin. God sent His only Son, Jesus, to live among us and demonstrate God's unconditional love. Though some religious leaders tried to distort His message, Jesus' death on the cross and resurrection ultimately conquered sin and death forever, and made the way for us to have eternal life with Him.

When Nicodemus heard what it meant to be born again, or have eternal life through Christ, he had to decide whether or not to accept what Jesus told him. Jesus wants all of us to be a part of His family. He not only told us—but showed us—by fulfilling the prophesies of His death and resurrection.

In this week's lesson students will get to consider the clear message of God's great love and the joy of being invited into His family.

Teacher Tips

○ Students will enjoy testing their communication skills in this simulation game.

○ It will be important to give the students a few minutes to practice the rules and get comfortable with them before you begin.

○ The debriefing questions will lead students to understand the clear message God has sent through His Word, and how that message is sometimes distorted by the world. You may want to also use this time at the end to invite students who may have never accepted God's salvation to talk to you or their parents about their faith in Jesus.

Supplies Needed

○ A bag of wrapped candy (or something else to use as rewards)

○ Slips of paper with instructions for the "parent"

Setup

○ Write each of the goals to be met on separate pieces of paper, fold, and place in a hat.

○ Select one student to act as the parent of the family. Give this student one of the following situations listed below. As the parent, he or she must communicate what is listed on the paper to the eldest, but the parent can use no words, only pantomime.

○ Select one student to act as the eldest. That student gives verbal instructions to the rest of the group, based on his or her interpretation of the parent's "charades." He or she may not ask the parent any questions. The rest of the group must follow the eldest's instructions.

○ Tell the parent that the reward can only be given after the goal is met.

○ After the first goal is reached, you may choose other pairs of students to be the parent and eldest, repeating the process for the second goal and so on.

○ Allow 10 to 15 minutes of simulation time.

GOALS TO BE MET

You must get all the students to stand on a chair.

You must get all the students to crawl under a table.

You must get all the students to sing "Happy Birthday."

You must get all the students to yell their favorite ice cream flavor on the count of three.

You must get all the students to close their eyes and touch their noses.

You must get all the students to touch their toes 10 times.

RULES TO LIVE BY

Discuss these rules before starting. You may want to write them out and post them at the front of the class.

① The parent can't speak or write any words.

② The eldest can't ask the parent any questions.

③ Group members can't ask questions of the eldest.

④ The only way to get the reward is by doing what the parent wants you to do.

SIMULATION

In a typical family, the children are expected to obey the parent or parents. Communication can be difficult enough in our busy world, but imagine what would happen if the parents' instructions, desires, and messages were mangled in the process. There are all kinds of obstacles that can get in the way of communication. If a parent had to work through the eldest child, for instance, the message to the rest of the family might end up confused or distorted. As a result, family members would end up doing the wrong things or wondering about how to reach a particular goal.

Let's see how well this imperfect system of family communication might work . . . or not work.

Begin the simulation by having the first student chosen as the parent try to communicate the goal to the eldest (without speaking), who will then tell the instruction to the class. The parent can only give a reward when all the students complete the desired action.

ANALYZING THE SITUATION

○ **How hard was it for you to understand what each goal was?** (*Answers will vary.*)

○ **What was the hardest thing about not being able to ask questions?** (*I didn't understand what was wanted, hard to follow directions, etc.*)

○ **What made it difficult for the parent to communicate?** (*he or she couldn't tell us, could only show us, etc.*)

○ **In what way is God like a loving parent?** (*He only wants the best for us, He has important information to give us, etc.*)

○ **What's the best way to learn what our loving Father wants us to do?** (*Ask Him directly and trust Him to show us, read His Word, listen to Him, etc.*)

○ **What obstacles can get in the way of understanding what God wants for our lives?** (*His message might be ignored, it might be twisted by people passing it along, it might be watered down by those receiving it, etc.*)

○ **What are some obstacles that keep people from understanding the clear message of God's plan for salvation?** (*People might not want to believe they are sinners, someone might have taught them wrong things about how to be saved, etc. Use this time to clearly articulate God's salvation plan, and invite those who aren't believers to accept Christ or bring their questions about salvation to you.*)

GOOD NEWS MULTIPLIES!

A communication activity illustrates the power of spreading the Gospel.

Bible Basis:
John 4:4–30, 39–42

Memory Verse:
I pray that you may be active in sharing your faith.
Philemon 1:6

BIBLE BACKGROUND

Rivalry and hatred prevailed between Jews and Samaritans during Jesus' day. Jesus was a Jew; the woman at the well was a Samaritan. She may have been surprised to see a Jewish man sitting at the well, but was even more surprised when He asked her for a drink!

The Son of God knew everything about this woman, and He looked beyond the external divisions to bring her a message that would transform her with living hope. He called her to worship in spirit and in truth. Jesus' model was a sharp contrast to the elitist sensibilities of the prevailing religious leaders. He was comfortable sharing hope with someone so decidedly different from Himself.

Your students have likely experienced cultural and communication differences in their own lives, and today's simulation illustrates the beauty of common hope among all people.

Teacher Tips

○ This game rewards those who can memorize things quickly and easily. If you have students who struggle with this skill, don't hold back your help! The purpose is to illustrate the cumulative effect of sharing the Gospel, not to punish kids who aren't able to memorize as easily.

○ If you don't have chairs, just sit in a circle on the floor.

○ The length of time required for this game depends on the number of students you have. If you have a particularly large group (more than 20), create an extra circle for each additional group of six to eight kids.

○ You might find it helpful to assign an adult leader to each circle who helps the kids.

Supplies Needed

○ *Optional:* chairs

Setup

○ Divide the number of kids in half, and arrange two circles of chairs at different sides of the room.

○ Assign an adult helper to assist each circle. It's important that kids don't add words about Jesus just to be funny or ridiculous. Adults should help kids choose biblical descriptors rather than random words.

RULES TO LIVE BY

Discuss these rules before starting. You may want to write them out and post them at the front of the class.

① You will sit with your original group unless you're asked to move.

② Each person will think of one word or simple phrase that describes Jesus.

③ You will try to remember each of your teammates' words in the order they were spoken.

SIMULATION

Imagine our class lives in two different countries. Half the class will live over here in Circle Land, and the other half lives over here on Round Island. You've never met or spoken to each other, but you both have very important things to share with each other.

We're going to see if it's possible for both countries to communicate to each other, until everyone in the class knows the same good news about Jesus. Those in each circle of chairs will begin spreading the good news in their own country first.

For example, the first person might say, "Jesus is my Savior!" The second person must repeat the first person's message, and then add his own to the list: "Jesus is my Savior AND He is holy!" The third person must repeat the first two, and then continue with a new message: "Jesus is my Savior, and He is holy, AND He loves me!" You'll continue until everyone in the circle can remember all the messages.

When you're confident that everyone has memorized the list, you'll pick a "missionary" representative to go to the other country and share your country's list. The other country is going to do the same, so even if you're not picked as the missionary, you'll wait and listen to their good news!

Assist kids as they begin to go around the circles, adding to the growing list of words or messages. Don't send a representative to the other country until both sides have had a chance to memorize their own list.

As a grand finale, see if someone from each circle can recite the other country's list.

ANALYZING THE SITUATION

○ **How did this activity help you remember good news?** *(Listen to students as they share.)*

○ **Some people keep good news all to themselves. Why is it important to share the Gospel with everyone in the world—and not just your own country?** *(It's clear that God asks us to go into the entire world to share the message of Jesus Christ. It's not given just to a special group of people!)*

○ **What would happen if someone added something untrue about Jesus? Why is it important to keep the message clear and consistent with what the Bible says about Jesus?** *(At this age, students can begin to understand truth—and the importance of biblical consistency. Point out that everyone can't just make up his own version of Jesus.)*

○ **What happens if one person tells 10 people about the Gospel, and then each of them tells 10 people? How does this kind of multiplication work?** *(Listen to kids' versions of the mathematical process. Draw an example of this on a board or piece of paper to illustrate the impact they can have.)*

BUILDING HIGHER

Accomplishing a frustrating group task teaches us to encourage one another.

Bible Basis:
John 5:1–15

Memory Verse:
May the God of hope fill you with all joy and peace as you trust in him, so that you may overflow with hope by the power of the Holy Spirit.
Romans 15:13

BIBLE BACKGROUND

The man at the pool of Bethesda must have felt hopeless and discouraged after 38 years on a mat all day. When Jesus approached this pool, He chose one of the most needy and despairing to heal and encourage. Jesus' command for the man to get up and walk demonstrated His authority. This healing resulted in a huge controversy with the religious leaders of the day since it went against their interpretation of the fourth commandment to keep the Sabbath holy.

We sympathize with the paralyzed man's discouragement. After all, he had sought healing for so long. The solutions he thought of seemed more and more impossible. But, hope remained, even though he didn't realize it at first. When the man accepted help from Jesus, he found healing. He learned a lesson worth remembering today: Jesus can help us when we're discouraged.

Sometimes we experience discouraging times in our families, work, or ministries. Just like Jesus met this paralyzed man who was disheartened, God can meet us in our difficult times. Persevering during those times requires the endurance that comes from God (Romans 15:5) as well as the encouragement that can come from fellow believers in Christ. We must look to Jesus, knowing that He can help us when we're discouraged.

TEACHER TIPS

○ Even though all groups receive the same instructions, they'll discover different ways to accomplish their building task. Allow them to fail without stepping in quickly to "rescue." This activity is designed to create some frustration, and the encouragement of teammates will keep them going.

○ If you don't have gumdrops available, you may use marshmallows.

○ Students are allowed to tape the ping-pong ball to the top of the tower.

○ Separate tables for each group are best, but you can set up several groups at one long table if necessary.

SUPPLIES NEEDED

○ Spaghetti noodles (the thicker the better)

○ A small bag of gumdrops for each group

○ Masking tape

○ Yardstick

○ Ping-pong balls (1 for each group)

SETUP

○ Form groups with three "architects" in each.

○ Ahead of time, establish a building site for each group on a clean, level surface.

○ Set out their materials: a handful of spaghetti noodles, a bag of gumdrops, and a ping pong ball.

RULES TO LIVE BY

Discuss these rules before starting. You may want to write them out and post them at the front of the class.

① You must use only the materials given to you.

② You must build the tallest tower you can in the time given.

③ The tower will be measured from its bottom to the top of the ping-pong ball.

④ You may break the spaghetti into different-sized pieces.

⑤ You may use masking tape to secure the ping-pong ball to the top of your tower.

SIMULATION

Have you ever considered how amazing architects are? They take materials and imagination and manage to design some pretty cool structures. I bet that when you showed up today, you didn't know you'd be an architect!

Your group has been given some simple materials with one goal in mind: design and build the tallest tower possible that will support a ping-pong ball on top. You might get discouraged sometimes, but keep trying! At the end of 15 minutes, we'll measure everyone's tower and see who built the tallest.

All right, architects . . . get going!

After the 15 minutes are up, and you've had time to measure everyone's tower, gather together to discuss the following questions.

ANALYZING THE SITUATION

○ **Was there anything discouraging about this fun activity? Did any of you feel like giving up?** *(Listen to the group share their experiences.)*

○ **How does discouragement affect our work?** *(Some students may observe that discouragement causes us to lose focus or get frustrated with our teammates. Sometimes we can even give up entirely.)*

○ **Was there anyone in your group who encouraged you to keep going?** *(This is a good opportunity to praise the positive students.)*

○ **The Bible is full of people who felt like giving up—people who were facing huge challenges. How does Jesus help us when we're discouraged and feel like giving up?** *(Listen to students' answers. Many will include friendships He provides, promises in the Bible, spiritual comfort, etc.)*

CASE FOR TRUTH

A mock trial exposes a false prophet.

Bible Basis:
John 8:56, 58; Isaiah 7:14; 9:6; Micah 5:2

Memory Verse:
In the beginning was the Word, and the Word was with God, and the Word was God. *John 1:1*

BIBLE BACKGROUND

Long before Jesus was born, the Jewish people were anticipating a Messiah. For over 2000 years, they'd been anxiously waiting for their deliverer to come free them. As each generation passed, hope of the Messiah's coming continued to build.

Predictions are often nothing more than informed guesses, but when they prove accurate time and time again, their truth is verified as more than just a guess. God used the prophets to foretell many of the details of Jesus' coming, yet many did not understand or see what had been promised. Even the disciples didn't understand the extraordinary things that were predicted long before Jesus' coming until well after the events occurred.

Emphasize to your students that God's promises are true— both when they are spoken and when we see the actual fulfillment of them. God is faithful to His promises, and all that He has spoken He will bring to pass.

TeACHeR TIPS

○ This simulation will run more smoothly if the teacher acts as the judge in this mock trial.

○ It's important to make sure all the evidence is in before the jury reaches a verdict. Some students with solid biblical background knowledge will recognize the real Isaiah right away, while others will have questions.

○ It will help if the lawyer and the two prophets are given the script to read through a few minutes ahead of time. Arrange the jury in separate chairs facing the two people on trial. They should not discuss their opinions until they hear the entire testimony.

SUPPLIES NeeDeD

○ Paper and pencil for jury members to take notes

○ *Optional:* gavel for the judge

SeTUP

○ Choose two serious and capable students to be the prophets. Secretly tell one of them that he or she is the real Isaiah. Instruct both that they'll give the answers provided to them, but they'll omit the scripture references (Isaiah #1) and correct answers (Isaiah #2).

○ Choose a capable lawyer to question the prophets. He or she should alternate the questions in bold between the two on trial.

○ The rest of the class is the jury. Their job will be to take all the evidence and decide who they think the real prophet is at the end of the trial.

○ Arrange the room to simulate a courtroom with jury seating, a witness stand, and a judge's seat. The lawyer will stand while he questions the prophets.

RULES TO LIVe BY

Discuss these rules before starting. You may want to write them out and post them at the front of the class.

① Jurors may take notes to get all the facts straight, but they must not discuss who they think the real prophet is until all the questions have been answered.

② Each person on the jury will get to give his or her vote at the end.

SIMULATION

Does anyone know what a prophet does? A prophet is someone God uses to speak His truth to others. God spoke to prophets telling them of Christ's birth long before He arrived. Many people believed the prophets, but some did not. There were also false prophets who would try to trick people into believing the wrong things for their own gain or who were simply misguided.

In this simulation you'll attempt to distinguish the truth in testimony. Let me introduce you to two people claiming to be the prophet Isaiah (introduce your two students). We also have a very capable lawyer here today who will question the two prophets on trial (introduce your lawyer). The rest of you are the jury, and you may not discuss your opinions until all the testimony has been heard.

I'll be the judge, so let's get started and see if the jury can find out who the real prophet is!

Proceed with the questioning. After all questions and answers are given, bring the jury together so they can discuss their opinions then vote on the person they think is the real Isaiah.

QUESTIONS FOR ISAIAH #1

1. What will the Messiah look like? Not anything great to look at. (Isa. 53:2)

2. What family tree will the Messiah be from? From David's line. (Isa. 9:6–7)

3. Where is the Messiah to be buried? In a rich man's grave. (Isa. 53:9)

4. What will His name be? Immanuel. (Isa. 7:14)

5. How will He respond when He is accused at His trial? He will stay silent. (Isa. 53:7)

QUESTIONS FOR ISAIAH #2

1. Where will the Messiah be born? In Jerusalem. (correct answer: Bethlehem)

2. What throne will He reign on? Egypt's throne. (correct answer: throne of David)

3. What will the Messiah come to do? To encourage people to get along and accept each other no matter what. (correct answer: restore man's relationship with God)

4. Will the Messiah be given a lot of power in the government? Yes, people in power and everyone else will obey Him. (correct answer: He'll be looked at with suspicion by the government—as a rebel and a troublemaker.)

5. How will the Messiah be treated? Like royalty. People will respect Him and honor him. (correct answer: He'll be hated and mistreated.)

ANALYZING THE SITUATION

○ **How did you know which prophet was telling the truth? Did you guess, or did you remember something from the Bible?** (*Allow students to share their answers.*) Let's look up some verses and see which "Isaiah" was really telling the truth. If you have time, look up the verses in Isaiah #1's answers.

○ **Why do you think people in Jesus' day didn't recognize the truth about what had already been written about Jesus?** (*They didn't know the Scriptures, He didn't act like the Messiah they expected, etc.*)

○ **How do you discern the truth about things people tell you?** (*I read God's Word, pray, ask for advice from other Christians, etc.*)

CENTURION SPIES ALIVE

The underground church watches for centurion spies as jail time is inevitable.

Bible Basis:
Philippians 1:12–13; 4:6–9

Memory Verse:
Your attitude should be the same as that of Christ Jesus.
Philippians 2:5

BIBLE BACKGROUND

Attitude counts. The apostle Paul had a lot of good reasons to have a bad attitude. This man was beaten, outcast, imprisoned, stoned, and rejected many times. Yet he continued to look up. He rejoiced even in great trials because he was sure God was working all things together for good. Paul chose to focus on God's grace and think of others instead of sinking into despair.

How many times are we in situations that are hard, unfair, or overwhelming? Paul shows us a great example of keeping our minds on Christ even when times are tough. Through Paul's rejoicing, many came to know Jesus Christ. Paul never lost hope because he knew he could depend on God, who would never leave him no matter what the circumstance.

Attitude does count. Others may see our joyful and thankful attitudes during hard times and wonder what strengthens us. This can lead to an opportunity to share about Christ. Encourage your tweens that as they rejoice always, they can show others the way to Christ.

TEACHER TIPS

○ The key to success for your selected spies is secrecy. Be sure to emphasize this for your students.

○ The Christians must find the hidden cross by following the clues you give them and then take it to the secret church location. If they're caught with the cross or caught searching alone, they can be taken to jail. Only the Christians will know where the church is located.

○ If the Romans find the secret church or get the cross first, they win. If the Christians get the cross to the secret church location, they win.

○ Set up clues for the Christians to follow by taping them under a table, behind a poster, etc. You'll hand them clue number one that should lead them to clue number two, and so on. You should have hidden four or five clues for the students to follow, leading the Christians to find a hidden cross drawn on a piece of paper.

SUPPLIES

○ Paper with a cross drawn on it

○ Four or five clues written on paper that eventually lead to the cross

○ Masking tape to designate the jail

○ Slips of paper with either *Romans* or *Christians* written on them (enough for all students in class)

○ Bowl or hat for students to draw their roles

SETUP

○ Hide a cross (drawn on a piece of paper) in your classroom or somewhere in the building where you meet. If the weather is nice, you can make this an outdoor activity.

○ Create a paper trail of clues to the location of the cross, much like a treasure hunt. Each clue will give directions to locate the next clue, with the final clue providing directions to the cross.

○ Use masking tape to mark off a square area or group chairs into a circle for the jail.

○ Divide the class into two groups, Romans and Christians, by letting students draw slips of paper from a bowl or hat.

○ The Romans must try to find the cross without the benefit of clues. The Romans can take the Christians to jail if they find the cross on them. They can also arrest a Christian if he or she isn't with another Christian, but they should not tell the Christian why he or she was arrested. (Secretly give the second reason for arrest to the Romans so the Christians don't know what it is.)

○ On two or three of the Romans' papers, write the word "spy" designating these students as secret Christians. The spies can let Christians go free from jail by touching their own ear. The jailer will need to watch for this signal to announce the Christians' release from prison.

○ The Christians must get together and secretly decide on a location for the church.

RULES TO LIVE BY

Discuss these rules before starting. You may want to write them out and post them at the front of the class.

① You must keep your roles secret.

② If a Roman takes you to jail, you must go willingly.

③ You may work together within your groups.

SIMULATION

Imagine we're back in biblical times. Some of you are Christians, some are Romans. The Romans must find Christians with the cross and take them to jail. There's one other specific reason the Romans may take Christians to jail. The Christians will have to figure out what that reason is if they are to avoid arrest. The Christians must follow the clues to find the cross and take it to a secret

church location that only they'll know. If the Romans find the cross, they win. If the Christians can get the cross to the church, they win.

The Christians should get together and decide on a location for the church and how they'll look for the cross. The Romans should pick a jailer. Allow a few minutes for students to gather within groups and decide on how they'll play.

Here's the first clue for the Christians. Hand them the first written clue.

You may begin. Allow 15–20 minutes for the game to play.

ANALYZING THE SITUATION

○ **What was unfair about this activity?** *(It seemed people were put in jail for no reason.)*

○ **How did you know who you could trust?** *(I had to watch what others did.)*

○ **When was it hard to have a good attitude?** *(when I was thrown into jail, etc.)*

○ **What was Paul's attitude like when he was in jail?** *(good, accepting, he worshiped God, etc.)*

○ **Why is having a good attitude important?** *(so others will see God in us, etc.)*

X-perience It! SCRIPTURE AND TOPIC INDEX

The following index allows you to use this book with any curriculum.
Simply find the Scripture your lesson is based on or the topic you are teaching.

Scripture	Topic	Page
Genesis 1:6–13	Creation by Design	6
Genesis 1:26—2:25	Uniqueness	10
Genesis 4:1–16	Pleasing God	14
Genesis 8:1—9:17	Grace/Provision	18
Genesis 13:11–12	Integrity	22
Genesis 18:1–5, 16–33	Integrity	22
Genesis 19:1–29	Integrity	22
Genesis 24	Guidance, Decision Making	26
Genesis 32:1—33:17	Peacemaking	30
Genesis 39:1—41:57	Attitude	34
Deuteronomy 6:4–7	Responsibility	38
2 Chronicles 29:1–19	Worship, Purity	42
2 Chronicles 30:1–27	Attitude, Trial	46
Psalm 104:24	Creation by Design	6
Isaiah 7:14	Truth, Trustworthiness	102
Isaiah 9:6	Truth, Trustworthiness	102
Isaiah 53:5–6	Truth, Trustworthiness	50
Jeremiah 36	Applying God's Word	54
Micah 5:2	Trustworthiness	102
Matthew 6:5–13	Communication, Prayer	58
Matthew 14:22–23	Sharing Your Faith, Courage	62
Matthew 15:21–28	Prayer, Persistence	66
Matthew 16:13–16	Acknowledging Who Jesus Is, Truth	50
Mark 1:29–31, 35–38	Needs/Wants	74
Mark 11:24	Prayer	66
Luke 2:1–20	Celebration	78
Luke 2:40–52	Responsibility	38
Luke 4:1–13	Applying God's Word, Choices, Temptation	82
Luke 11:1–13	Prayer, Pursuing God	70
Luke 18:1–8	Prayer, Pursuing God	70
Luke 19:1–10	Needs/Wants	74
Luke 24:13–35	Sharing Your Faith	86
John 3:1–16	Salvation by Grace	90
John 4:4–30, 39–42	Faith, Sharing Your Faith, Urgency	94
John 4:21, 24	Worship	42
John 5:1–15	Discouragement	98
John 8:56, 58	Truth, Trustworthiness	102
John 14:13-14	Prayer, Asking	66
Philippians 1:12–13	Persecution	106
Philippians 4:6–9	Persecution	106
1 John 4:14–15	Acknowledging Who Jesus Is	50

X-perience It! CORRELATION CHART

Each activity correlates to a Unit and Lesson in the curriculum lines shown below.
For further help on how to use the chart see page 5.

Title	Page	Scripture Reference	David C. Cook BIL LifeLINKS to God College Press Reformation Press Wesley Anglican	Echoes The Cross
Hey! You Did That on Purpose!	6	Genesis 1:6–13; Psalm 104:24	Unit 1, Lesson 2	Unit 1, Lesson 2
Super Statues!	10	Genesis 1:26—2:25	Unit 1, Lesson 4	Unit 1, Lesson 4
It's All Mine, Baby!	14	Genesis 4:1–16	Unit 2, Lesson 6	Unit 2, Lesson 6
Plan-it Planet	18	Genesis 8:1—9:17	Unit 2, Lesson 8	Unit 2, Lesson 8
Stand Alone	22	Genesis 13:11–12; 18:1–5, 16–33; 19:1–29	Unit 3, Lesson 10	Unit 3, Lesson 10
We All Live in a Yellow Submarine	26	Genesis 24	Unit 3, Lesson 12	Unit 3, Lesson 12
Case for Truth	102	John 8:56, 58; Isaiah 7:14; 9:6; Micah 5:2	Unit 4, Lesson 1	Unit 4, Lesson 1
Bethlehem Barter	78	Luke 2:1–20	Unit 4, Lesson 3	Unit 4, Lesson 3
Responsibility Rocks	38	Deuteronomy 6:4–7; Luke 2:40–52	Unit 5, Lesson 5	Unit 5, Lesson 5
I Gotta Have It!	82	Luke 4:1–13	Unit 5, Lesson 7	Unit 5, Lesson 7
Westward Ho!	74	Mark 1:29–31, 35–38; Luke 19:1–10	Unit 5, Lesson 9	Unit 5, Lesson 9
Get Outta Your Zone!	62	Matthew 14:22–33	Unit 6, Lesson 11	Unit 6, Lesson 11
Building Higher	98	John 5:1–15	Unit 6, Lesson 13	Unit 6, Lesson 13
Can You Hear Me Now?	90	John 3:1–16	Unit 7, Lesson 2	Unit 7, Lesson 2
Who Am I?	50	Isaiah 53:5–6; Matthew 16:13–16; 1 John 4:14–15	Unit 7, Lesson 4	Unit 8, Lesson 8
Bible Smugglers	86	Luke 24:13–35	Unit 8, Lesson 6	Unit 8, Lesson 7
Good News Multiplies	94	John 4:4–30, 39–42	Unit 8, Lesson 8	Unit 7, Lesson 3
Ice Cream—You Scream!	30	Genesis 32:1—33:17	Unit 9, Lesson 10	Unit 8, Lesson 10
Jail Jurisdiction	34	Genesis 39:1—41:57	Unit 9, Lesson 12	Unit 9, Lesson 12
Trash to Treasure	42	2 Chronicles 29:1–19; John 4:21, 24	Unit 10, Lesson 1	Unit 10, Lesson 1
Bricks and Mortar	46	2 Chronicles 30:1–27	Unit 10, Lesson 3	Unit 10, Lesson 3
Bridging the Gap	58	Matthew 6:5–13	Unit 11, Lesson 5	Unit 11, Lesson 5
A Knight's Tale (Week One)	66	Matthew 15:21–28; Mark 11:24; John 14:13–14	Unit 11, Lesson 7	Unit 11, Lesson 7
A Knight's Tale (Week Two)	70	Luke 11:1–13; 18:1–8	Unit 11, Lesson 9	Unit 11, Lesson 9
Time Warp!	54	Jeremiah 36	Unit 12, Lesson 11	Unit 12, Lesson 11
Centurion Spies Alive	106	Philippians 1:12–13; 4:6–9	Unit 12, Lesson 13	Unit 12, Lesson 13

INSTRUMENT PANEL QUESTIONS

Document your decisions for the journey in the space provided.

① You're heading toward a patch of sea kelp that you must go through. There's no other way. If your propellers get caught in the kelp you may be stuck forever. What should you do? Read Mark 13:33. Find the two instructions that will help you get through the area in your submarine. Write them below.

_____   _____

② You must choose between two paths. One way is a wide bay; the other is a narrow, difficult channel. Which way should you go? Read Matthew 7:13–14 to find out. Write your answer here.

_____

③ You see a large clam on the ocean floor and you can be sure it will have a valuable pearl inside, but it might not be easy to get. Read Matthew 13:45–46 to find out what you should do. Write your answer below.

_____

④ A great enemy ship is attacking you from above. Should you shoot back or leave quickly and trust your backup boats to take care of the problem? Read 1 Peter 2:23 and record your answer below.

_____

⑤ Your submarine loses power. Lights go off and you're sitting dead in the water. How can you receive more power to finish your journey? Read Acts 1:8 and write your answer below.

_____

When you've finished your journey, you may exit your submarine.